Riding with
REAGAN

Contents

Riding with
REAGAN

1

The Bond Is Forged

I was in what we called the down room in the White House, taking a break with a few other agents, when my shift leader came in to ask if any of us could ride. The down room is a small room near the command post with a few couches and some hooks on the wall where the agents can hang their jackets. The shift leaders had been asking all the agents the same question, "Does anyone know how to ride a horse?" At first, the question surprised me, but I sheepishly raised my hand. The boss said, "Barletta, you're going to go over to President-elect Reagan's detail out at the ranch next time."

I said in response, "Yes, sir."

Consisting of approximately two thousand agents, the U.S. Secret Service is an integrated but layered network. In its sophisticated operations, the Secret Service assigns each division with a specific area of protection. The Uniformed Division is responsible for the security of the White House and grounds, as well as foreign embassies in the United States. They outfit their command post with equipment such as infrared cameras that monitor all that is going on in or near the White House. They are usually a part of the Secret Service advance team in charge of the magnetometers, dog teams, and countersniper teams. The Technical Security Division (TSD) makes certain all the electronic systems are in place, including the ground's perimeter alarms.

Located in the West Wing of the White House, the surprisingly unpretentious Secret Service command post is referred to as W-16. When compared to the Uniformed Division, the equipment is simple—a few television monitors and a switchboard to receive incoming calls. Today it is much more sophisticated, with the supervisors' offices and plenty of state-of-the-art technology located across the street in the Executive Office Building. In this mammoth operation, everyone has a boss—supervisors, shift leaders, and working agents. On our detail, everyone answered to the shift leader first.

The entire Secret Service always faces a huge learning curve during the transition to a new administration. Following the election of a new president, the Presidential Protective Division (PPD) splits the detail between the sitting president and the president-elect so that some agents can start getting used to the new man's needs and mannerisms. Right from the beginning, President Reagan's detail started accompanying him to his ranch. With the grueling campaign over, the ranch was where he and Mrs. Reagan wanted to go to relax.

It soon became apparent that the supervisors at the ranch were having quite a time finding agents to protect the newly elected president while he was riding his horse. Horses are dangerous, and you have to know what you are doing. The rider is handling a big animal weighing about twelve hundred pounds with incredible strength and jumping and running abilities and with a brain the size of a walnut.

The problems at the ranch began even before anyone mounted a horse. First, no one had any idea how to tie a horse, the president-elect ended up saddling the horses for the agents. Things only got worse once they started riding. President Reagan would ride fast and jump fences. He was really an English equestrian rider. The agents assigned to him did not know how to ride, and they were having trouble keeping up with him. One day, an agent fell off his horse and broke his arm. The president-elect dismounted his horse to take care of the agent. Our chief supervisor at the time rightly said that was not how things should work. The President was not supposed to be giving us aid and comfort. That was what we should be doing for him.

After that incident, the detail supervisor called the White House and said, "I have a big problem out here. I need someone who can ride a horse." The supervisor at the White House put out the word to the shift leaders that they needed to find an agent who could *really* ride. And that's where I came in.

To DEAL WITH the new security needs at the ranch following Reagan's election, the Secret Service created the Western Protective Division (WPD), which would protect the ranch even when the First Couple was not there. In the weeks before the inauguration, agents made a trip to Santa Barbara, California. Members of the Secret Service always fly commercially unless they are working a shift. Only then do they fly on *Air Force One* or another government aircraft.

In Santa Barbara, the agents used dozens of rental cars that had been brought up from Los Angeles. During the first few months, we drove those rental cars from our hotel in Santa Barbara to the ranch for our eight-hour shifts, but the drive up the winding mountain road was tough, and it wasn't long before sturdier Chevy Suburbans replaced them. For the next eight years, the Suburbans were workhorses, transporting the agents on those precipitous drives to and from the ranch. The number of agents on duty at the ranch varied, depending on ever-changing circumstances such as the weather and the President's arrivals and departures. In addition to the dog teams outside the perimeter, there could be as many as fifty-four supplemental agents standing post.

The President and I first met in late November 1980 during my first trip to the ranch. On my first morning there, I was standing outside the barn with Jerry Parr, the deputy special agent in charge, when the president-elect approached us on his way to get his horse ready. A path of about fifty steps led from the ranch house to the tack room.

Built on a hill, the tack room was in a metal and brick building with two large rooms. In one of the rooms were the President's two Jeeps, a tractor, and all the ranch tools, including chain saws, pole saws, and axes. All the horse equipment was kept inside the second room, where the wall was covered with saddles hanging on racks. Some of the saddles were gifts that the President had received, while others were ones he had used for years. Near the tack room was a workbench attached to the wall, which was used for taking chain saws apart. The stables were next to the barn, and they were usually empty because the President liked to let his horses run free.

Reagan was dressed to go riding; he had on his jodhpurs, one of the three shirts he always wore, and the best English riding boots, brown Dehner three-buckle field boots from Omaha. These boots were from the old school, and few people wear them anymore.

The President saw us and said, "Good morning."

"Good morning, Mr. President," Jerry responded. "This is agent John Barletta. He is from the White House detail, and he is going to ride with you today." A quiet, soft-spoken, intelligent man, Jerry looked like Walter Matthau. All the shift members liked him, and their respect for him was immense. He was highly experienced and really knew his job.

The President nodded and smiled, but you could tell by the look in his eyes that he was skeptical. *Oh no*, he was thinking, *not another one that I am going to have to babysit. I won't be able to do what I want, because these guys can't ride.*

My boss knew nothing about horseback riding, and he had never seen me ride either. Still, Jerry was anxious to give me a try. Before we went into the tack room, he gave me explicit instructions on how to handle the president-elect and his requests while riding with him. "John, the President may ask you if it's all right for him to do something while riding. Always tell him that he can do whatever he wants to do and that you will keep up with him."

"Mr. Parr," I reminded him, "you've never seen me on a horse. You don't even know if I can ride or not."

Jerry shot back, "You told me you could!"

When we entered the barn, the President was expecting to gather his tack (saddle, bridle, halter, and cleaning gear). There were usually six horses at the ranch. President Reagan was a very particular rider, and he knew just how he wanted the slipknot for his horse tied. He also wanted his saddle positioned and secured in just a certain way. The horse's shape determines the exact placement of the saddle, and the front of the saddle needs to fit over his withers, the place where the neck comes into the shoulder of the horse. Some horses do not have good withers, making it extremely difficult to secure a saddle on them. When you tighten the saddle, it needs to be done just right. If it is too tight, the horse will have difficulty breathing, and if it is not tight enough, it will come loose while you are riding. Cinching a saddle properly takes some practice.

The President usually got his own horse ready. For the most part, good riders want to saddle their own horses, but on my first morning there, I wanted everything just right, so I had tacked up his horse before he got to the barn.

I followed him to his horse, and I could tell he was surprised that the horse was ready. I had groomed the horse, picked his feet, put his halter on, lifted his stirrups, and placed the saddle on securely. Of course, I was nervous as he started looking his horse over. Soon I heard him say, "Now John, I want to show you a couple of things. I like to tie my horses this way," but when he looked at the slipknot, he realized that I knew how to do that. "Oh, I see you've done that before."

Then he talked about the way the saddles are positioned. "Now, John, my saddle—Oh, I see you've done that before too."

When he lifted one of the horse's hooves to clean it and saw that it had already been done, he just said, "Oh, my, my." Following a few such observations by the President, I could see that he had a little bit more trust in me, but after all he had seen over the past few weeks, he was still leery.

Ready to go, we mounted our horses and started walking them. The President rode a big, black thoroughbred mare that he had raised himself. Since the Secret Service had not obtained any of its own horses yet, I rode one of the President's— Gwalianko, a beautiful gray. The weather that morning was bright and seasonable. It is usually seventy-five degrees and sunny in Santa Barbara in November, but the weather at the ranch can be more variable. On that morning, it was close to perfect. As we rode toward the tiny adobe ranch house, painted white with a red Spanish-tiled roof, it looked as if it was just a small part of a painting under the vast blue sky. The land was flat where the house was built, but from that spot, there was a panoramic view of the mountain range and the groves of imposing oak trees.

As we passed the house and entered the pasture, the President asked, "Can we pick up the pace and trot?"

"Mr. President," I said, "you can do anything you want."

We started trotting; it was a test. If I could not have kept up, he probably would have stopped, as he had done in the past with the other agents, but I stayed right with him, and soon we were in the field. The grass was swaying, and the field looked like a green ocean. We continued trotting, and before I knew it, we were talking. He started calling me John right away. Although mindful of my purpose in riding with the President, I was at ease with him, and there were moments when I almost forgot that this was our first ride together.

If you're not a good rider, your butt slaps the saddle as soon as you start trotting. The President kept watching me closely, and he noticed that I wasn't slapping the saddle. He looked at me and smiled.

When we reached a fence, we needed to open the gate. Along the path we were riding on, the gates had been left closed but unlocked. Once the ride was over, however, they were again secured by a combination lock. It is dangerous to lean over the horse and undo the latch. Not wanting me to have to open it, the President leaned right over his horse and said, "John, I'll get it."

"No, Mr. President, I will get that for you." Instead of leaning over the horse, I sidestepped my horse up to the gate and undid the latch. Again he looked at me, but this time he gave me one of those big Irish smiles that goes right through you.

After I had opened the gate, and we had ridden through it, he asked me, "John, do you want me to close the gate?"

"No, Mr. President," I said. "There is a vehicle full of agents behind us. We need to leave it open. They will close the gate."

Most of the ground at the ranch is hard and rocky. Once you get beyond the first gate, there is a nice, soft stretch across the meadow that goes down for about a mile before you get to the well. Here, the President wanted to run. "John, do you mind if we do a collected canter?" he asked, the reins firmly in his hands.

"Mr. President," I answered, "you can do anything you want."

When you do a collected canter, the horse is moving out, but not in a full run. When you canter—a moderate gallop—each horse usually tries to compete with the other. That's much harder than it looks. If you don't know what you're doing, the horse will run away with you. We started cantering, and the horses were running side by side. Anybody who rides knows how difficult that is to do. It's extremely unusual for the horses to remain next to each other. Our horses, though, matched strides, equal with each other.

We kept the horses at the same stride for about fifteen minutes until we got to the well. The President raised his hand and said, "Whoa!" just like someone in the cavalry would say it.

From the well, he liked to turn off into the brush, which was about two miles from where we started. There was a new well constructed by the U.S. Navy Seabees. The older well on the President's property was called the beehive, and it provided the water for the ranch.

After Reagan was elected president, big changes were needed to accommodate the additional people working there. No longer would just the Reagans and maybe a few friends and family be at the ranch. Instead, there could be 175 people at any one time. There were agents, special officers, Secret Service Uniformed Division dog teams, countersniper teams, and so on. To help secure the place, twenty-nine Secret Service vehicles were kept on the property. They had to build a helicopter pad for *Marine One* and a hangar to store it in. In addition, a plane was on-site that nobody knew about—nor would they, unless it was needed. It is hard to imagine that all of this was going on when you see the pictures of the President out for his private, peaceful rides on the trails. The agents did all they could to shelter the First Couple from intrusions, so that they could enjoy their time alone. Trees and shrubs were planted to cover many of the buildings, giving them a sense of privacy.

The brush area past the well was rocky and full of trees, and the trails were hidden by vegetation, including madrone trees, oaks, and greasewood. Looking down into the valley, you felt that you were on top of the world as you took in the moss-covered rocks, grand oak trees, and patches of twisted vines and roots. For the President, it was almost a sacred area—a place of complete solace from huge demands and decisions. While riding here, we saw many gophers scurrying around. It seemed like there were millions of them. People who love horses hate gophers, since they not only ruin the vegetation, but they make holes that could cause a horse to break a leg if he steps into one. Eight years later, I found out how dangerous those could be.

We rode together for another two hours on these narrow, roaming trails. The President didn't say a word, and I wouldn't think of starting a conversation unless I had to inform him of something. I would always wait to speak until after he'd spoken to me. I knew my place and didn't want to take advantage of my position.

Once we had entered the brush area, we lost the vehicle carrying the other agents. The agents kept calling me, wanting to know how we were doing and what was going on. After a number of these calls, I told them to reduce the radio traffic unless necessary so that I could concentrate.

When we arrived back at the house, we went to the hitching post, where Jerry was watching for us. He looked worried, his brow all crinkled up, and he waited for the President to get off his horse so he could ask him a question. The President always dismounted his horse by throwing his right leg over the saddle and jumping down, which is extremely dangerous. Most people dismount by throwing their right leg over the horse's rump, but I could never talk him out of it. He did it from day one.

While the President was tying up his horse to the hitching post, Jerry asked him, "How did it go, Mr. President? How was your ride?"

President Reagan first looked at me and then turned back to my boss. "Well, you finally got me a good one," he said.

2

The Unlikeliest of Friends

That first ride was the beginning of a special relationship that was forged through not only a love for horses but the many years we spent riding over the trails alone. My boss made it clear to me on that sunny November morning that from then on, I had to be prepared to come out to the ranch every time the President did, and I would go with him anywhere else he was going to ride.

There were things about Ronald Reagan I already knew I liked. The first time I saw him and heard him speak was on October 28, 1980, in Cleveland, Ohio, at the Bond Court Hotel. For members of the Secret Service, a presidential campaign always presents challenges and changes. After Robert Kennedy was assassinated in the kitchen of the Ambassador Hotel in Los Angeles, California, in 1968, Congress decreed that the Secret Service must cover any viable candidate running for president. Five individuals from different areas of the government determine viability. Once a candidate is deemed viable, he or she starts to have the aura of the presidency, because it's a lot bigger deal if a candidate shows up with a Secret Service entourage than if they just ride up in a taxi.

I was on the detail covering President Carter at one of the debates, and I was impressed by the way Reagan handled himself. I remember how much I liked it when he kept saying, "Well, there you go again," and then there was the "Are you better off now than you were four years ago?" line. Of course we weren't, with fifty-seven hostages in Iran and 21 percent interest rates.

After that debate, I remember hearing one of President Carter's aides tell him, "Mr. President, you did a great job."

"I did not," was all he said in response. Everyone, including President Carter, knew Reagan had eaten him up.

Those unforgettable lines from the debates were only the first of many endearing things I would hear from Reagan. He was likable from the beginning, and he really knew how to communicate. His vision for America was optimistic. I had previously covered both President Ford's son Michael and his wife Gayle and, then, President Carter. During those years the country was struggling, and consequently, many Americans were pessimistic about the future. Now there would be a new man in the White House. His ideas were hopeful—things could be good again, and there were opportunities for everyone. As we learned over the years, those were not just his ideas, but beliefs he held dearly.

BECAUSE OF HIS UPBRINGING, the glitz of Hollywood and the power of the White House did not reveal much about the man I came to know. Reagan valued decency and hard work and found respite in the simple pleasures of life. Reagan's core came from his mother, Nelle Reagan. As I got to know him, it became clear that his mother ran the house when he was growing up. Jack Reagan, his father, was an alcoholic who worked as a shoe salesman, most of the time holding small jobs while always on the search for his pot of gold. The family spent years bouncing around Illinois, and as a boy, Reagan never lived in a house that his family owned. Instead, he grew up in apartments above a bank and later a shoe store, as well as various rental homes along the way. Before reaching his teen years, he lived in five different towns and twelve rented apartments or houses. He was often the new kid on the block. Seeking comfort from the difficulties all those childhood disruptions must have caused, he gravitated more to his mother, who was his anchor.

His mother set all the rules and made all the critical decisions for her boys. When Reagan became a father, he would tell his children to go to their mother when they had a problem or a difficult question, because that is how he had seen it done. Clearly, his mother taught him the values for which he came to be admired—being down to earth, being idealistic, and telling it like it is. He got all that from Nelle Reagan.

His father, who could be cynical, had very little influence on him, and his brother, Neil (or "Moon") Reagan, had even less influence on him. He used to call Neil the "One-Match Kid" because he was a chain-smoker. Neil would light a cigarette, and then before that cigarette would go out, he'd use it to light another one, chain-smoking all day. To Reagan, that habit was a mystery.

Early on in our relationship, the President put me at ease. While riding our horses, I was always conscious of my duty: to protect him. Still, on those early rides, I was surprised by how disarming and transparent he was with me.

Once, after we had been riding for some time in silence, he asked me, "John, you know the best job I ever had?"

I thought I knew the answer to that one, so I immediately answered, "Yes, sir, being president."

"No," he replied. "I was a dishwasher in a girl's sorority." As he explained it, he could stand around all those pretty girls and get paid for it!

In fall 1928, just a year before the Depression, Reagan left Dixon, Illinois, to enroll in Eureka College. A poor young man, it was extremely difficult for him not only to get into school but then to pay for it once he was there. He worked hard, though, taking side jobs. His work ethic, which he inherited from his mother, ran deep. While still living in Illinois, he also worked as a salesman at a sporting goods store. He liked that job, and he told me that at one time he thought that was what he would do for a living.

Reagan's humble upbringing kept him modest throughout his life. When he combined his work ethic with his natural good looks and charm, it didn't take him long to land some starring roles in Hollywood. However, he didn't have an ego. I never heard him say, "I can do that because I'm president of the United States." While he was a part of Hollywood and the whole system, it never became a big part of him. Anyone who has watched his movies can see how his plain mannerisms came out on the screen, just as they did in his politics. People wanted to sit and listen to him.

His actions and choices were unlike many of the other stars and climbers around him. Countless Hollywood marriages have broken up because the success of one partner has bruised the other's ego, but not Reagan. He ended up divorced from Jane Wyman, because she'd just won an Oscar for her performance in *Johnny Belinda*, while he was busy making B movies. He didn't care, but obviously she did, and Wyman filed for the divorce. That devastated him, and he never talked about it later in life.

President Reagan never put on airs. He had a remarkable ability to be just as comfortable with the person cutting his hair as he was with actor Charlton Heston, who was one of his very good friends from their days in the Screen Actors Guild. Once, when we were riding along a trail, he started to tell me about *Santa Fe Trail*, a movie he had made with Errol Flynn in 1940. I had always been curious about Flynn, and while I would never have been the one to initiate a conversation like this one with him, I seized the opportunity to ask the President a question about the movie star. "Are all the stories about his womanizing true?"

"John," he said, "I went out with him for three nights, and I couldn't keep up with him. He'd be up all night and then on the set the next day, his lines all memorized and ready to go, looking good. He was a true professional."

The President was good-looking and naturally had many women after him, so I've been told. Yet he never would have bragged about it. I asked him, "I understand you were sought after too?"

"Well, I guess a little bit," he said and smiled. While he wouldn't elaborate, his friends sure told me. He was just too humble to brag.

The President was also graceful and a good slow dancer, but he wasn't musical. I remember him singing in church once, and you wouldn't want him in the choir. I never saw any records around or heard any music on his radio. I once asked him if he wanted the radio on in the limousine, and he said, "No." I later asked him one or two times more, and then I dropped it. When he said "No," that was exactly what he meant.

As I got to know the President better, his honesty impressed me greatly. Although in many ways he was smooth and always seemed a bit like a Hollywood leading man, he was forthright. That puzzled his critics. Some people say he wasn't the smartest president. Maybe he wasn't, but he knew his facts. His memory was phenomenal. He would read the scripts for the promotional videos shot at his office in Century City after his presidency, and he would always get them in one take. The producers and the directors couldn't believe it. I remember one time they asked him, "Okay, Mr. President, can we do it again?"

"Why? Did I do something wrong?"

"No, no, it was great."

"Then why are we going to do it again?" he asked.

They looked at each other for reassurance, and then someone would say, "Well, I guess we don't have to do it again. Yeah, that's perfect." Some of the President's friends called him "One-Shot Reagan."

Even more than knowing his facts, he knew and understood people and human nature. Early on, he came to appreciate the fact that I knew my limitations—and everyone has plenty of them. I had only been to the ranch a few times when an incident took place. It illustrated to me just how well he understood that pride was one of the worst human vanities. One morning a military aide had a problem with his horse, so the President let him use one of his. Seeing that the aide was having a few problems readying the horse, I walked over to him and asked, "Sir, can I help you with your horse?"

He looked at me and answered, "I was born in Corpus Christi, Texas. I've been riding horses for years."

I continued to watch him for a few more moments and saw that he was still struggling. "Okay, fine," I said as I walked away.

Next, the President came up. He was on his way to get Mrs. Reagan's horse, No Strings, which was always the first part of his routine. He got the saddle and the grooming equipment and then started brushing her horse. He noticed right away what was going on, and he looked over at the military aide and then at me. I said, "Sir, I tried to give him some assistance. He told me he knows everything about horses. He grew up in Texas." Not a word was said, but the President saw what I saw, the aide had put the saddle pad on incorrectly.

When the President was finished with No Strings, he next went to get his horse, El Alamein, a big gray Arabian thorough-bred. As he walked El Alamein over to where he had put his grooming equipment, he looked at the military aide again. The aide was now trying to put the bit in the horse's mouth, and he had gotten it upside down and backwards. The horse was throw-ing his head, so the President tied up El Alamein and looked at me again over El Alamein's back. I just shrugged my shoulders.

Finally he said, "John, he's going to hurt my horse."

"Yes, sir."

"Well, I'm going to have to say something."

Normally, he would never do that, but it was unsafe. Since I had already tried to help the aide, I was not going to go over there again.

The horse was still fussing and pitching his head as the

President walked over to the aide. He politely asked him, "Excuse me. May I show you something?" He then took the bridle out of the aide's hands, straightened it out, put the bit into the horse's mouth, and the head stall around his ears. The horse started licking his lips as contented as could be.

Instead of saying, "Thank you, Mr. President, I appreciate it," the aide said, "I knew there was something wrong with the equipment." No one else said a word.

Not only was Reagan right about the bit, but he was the president of the United States, and it was *his* horse. He was just too polite to inform the aide that there was nothing wrong with the equipment.

MY LIFE, TOO, had a humble beginning. I was in the middle of five kids, and my father was a police officer. While the most money I think he ever made in a year was twenty-five thousand dollars, he provided for our large family. In retrospect, I'm amazed at how my father actually did it. I don't remember ever wanting for anything. I don't remember ever going hungry. I don't remember being unable to see a movie. The family always had a vehicle.

Like the President, I had a wonderful mother. There were also some other women who loomed large in my formative years. Primarily, they were the Sisters of St. Joseph's Order at St. Clement, a Catholic school, who taught me from grades one through twelve. I know for certain that I never would have accomplished as much as I have, whatever that may be, without being taught by the nuns. I still remember all of them—especially Sister Diaonysia.

We received corporal punishment from the nuns, and we

needed it. Today if children went home and told their fathers that some nun hit them, there would be lawsuits flying. In my day, though, my father would hit me again for making the nun hit me.

Although we lived in Somerville, Massachusetts, which is right next to Boston, we attended St. Clement that was actually in Medford. Every day, I walked to school, as did my three brothers and one sister. We were years apart in age, but we all went to St. Clement at one time or another. Ed and Bob were five years older than I was, while Barbara was five years younger. My mother gave birth to my youngest brother, Chuck, when she was forty-five years old.

About thirty-five students stayed together all through those twelve years. In some ways, it was just like the movies that portray what school used to be like. There were inkwells in the desks, and the boys would dip the pigtails of the girl in front of them into the ink. The boys had to wear a suit or a sports jacket, a white shirt, and a tie every day, and the girls wore navy blue uniforms with white-collared blouses. Even then there was pressure to have the latest styles, so having a specific dress code took some financial strain off my parents. My mother passed the white shirts that my brothers had worn down to me. The dress code at St. Clement was based on the assumption that people act differently, depending on how they are dressed. While that is true to some extent, we would still tussle around, and now and again I would damage a sports jacket. The school yard we played on was cement, and things could get rough.

My relationship with my father was markedly different from the one Reagan had with his. In my life, my father played an important role. Although both of us had saintly moms, my mother's word wasn't as final as Nelle Reagan's. My parents would talk about things. Even though my father had so many responsibilities, he still found the time to be my Little League baseball coach. He was a strong figure, and not only did he have a great reputation as a police officer and detective, but he had arrested many of the mafia-type figures from Boston.

Like Reagan, I had an early love affair with horses. Most of the time, I'd get to ride only if I could save enough money to rent a horse from the Pony Boy Stables near my home, but one of my biggest thrills was when my father would take me with him to the Boston Mounted Police. They had a stable right in downtown Boston, and at the age of ten, the officers down there would let me ride one of the horses in the ring. That was what got me hooked. Many people are unaware of Boston's rich history with horses, thoroughbreds in particular. The United States Equestrian Olympic Team works out in the Boston area. In Boston, everyone rides English.

After St. Clement, I first went into the military service before I enrolled in college. I enlisted in the U.S. Army and was in what they called Airborne Unassigned—which was really stupid. Back then, most people in the military didn't even have a high school education. Many of them ended up there. It was either go there or go to jail. Of course, it's quite different today, but that was in 1962, and it was a huge eye-opener for me. I could've gone into other fields of the military, joining the "white-shirt army" and pushing papers somewhere. In fact, my father tried to talk me into going into an area in which I could use my education, but I didn't heed his advice. Instead, I was in the mud airborne infantry, because that was what I wanted to do.

The President knew of my military service, but we hardly ever talked about it. He couldn't go into the service as a combat soldier in the Second World War because of his poor eyesight, and he had to watch his friends like Jimmy Stewart enter the combat arena. He idolized Stewart, who became a general. I think the President was disappointed that he never got his chance, but he never complained that he couldn't go overseas. He told me, "I tried to go into combat, but I couldn't. I've always had bad eyesight." He was also deaf in one ear from pistols going off. During one of our rides, he told me how while filming one of the movies, a stuntman held a gun right up to his ear and then fired it. He lost a lot of his hearing from that incident.

Following the military, I went on to Boston College, where I was taught by the brothers. I was there for two years, but completed just one year of studies because I went part-time at night. Each evening after classes I drove to Logan Airport where I worked as a flight information coordinating agent for TWA. At the time, I was the youngest person to work in that position for TWA. After those two years, I transferred to the University of Arizona where I finished my college work.

One thing that Reagan and I shared in common as young men is that we both saw going to college as an immense privilege. Financially, it was a struggle for both of us. When I came back from the military, I was able to go to college on the G.I. Bill, which gave me one hundred seventy-five dollars a month. I lived on campus, and because I was a little older when I went to college, I truly appreciated it.

I really started my heavy riding while I was going to college in Arizona, where I met Mr. Kelly. He was like a thin John

Wayne, and he ran a horseback-riding facility. He rolled his own cigarettes, wore a cowboy hat, and was a natural around horses. He had a lovely wife and young kids.

I wanted to ride, but I couldn't afford to rent his horses. "I'll tell you what," he said. "I've seen you ride, and I could use your help. When people come in, you take them out for a ride, whether they want to go for an hour or two. Then you can have the pick of any horse you want to ride for nothing." He just liked the way I handled horses and my way with them.

This ranch was out in the desert. Riding in Arizona was different from Boston—no cobblestones, but plenty of cactus. In the Arizona desert, a type of cactus grows called jumping cactus, which looks like a spiny round fish, and I learned quickly that the horses would always get the jumping cactus in their feet. To deal with this problem, I started carrying a comb with me. Using the wide edge of the comb, I would stick it on the horse and pull the cactus spines off his foot.

I began taking groups out for rides. Before I took anyone out I'd ask, "Do you want to trot? Can you trot? Do you want to run? Can you run? If you are running, you have very little room for error." Most people would exaggerate their riding skills. (Later, even the Secret Service agents would inflate their abilities with horses.) However, this wasn't too hard for me to figure out. As soon as we reached the stables, I could tell who could really ride. I'd always go over it with them again and say, "Don't tell me you know how to ride if you don't, because I'm going to give you a horse to match your ability. If you don't know how to ride that well, then I will give you an easier horse." Usually the guys trying to impress their girlfriends were the ones who exaggerated their abilities, but I said, "You can get hurt out there."

One of my first rides was with a group of ten. Mr. Kelly's son rode drag, keeping everyone together. After the ride, I went to Mr. Kelly and asked, "How did I do?"

"John," he said, "you did great. Everybody liked you, but would you please learn how to pronounce horse? They're not *hosses*. They're *horses*. When you start using words like that, the people start doubting that you can ride." He reassured me, however, that in spite of my Boston accent, the minute I did start to ride, it was obvious I knew what I was doing.

I stole away to ride whenever I could. I'd go up into the hills by myself, wearing my Army field jacket with the insulated liner. My friends would harass me asking, "Where the hell are you going with all that cold weather gear?" I guess those guys forgot that I was going from the ninety-degree Arizona heat to about a forty-degree temperature up in the hills. I'd sleep overnight on a saddlebag, just like in the movies. It was my kind of fun.

During my early riding days in the late 1960s, Reagan already owned a ranch. By that time, he had established his habit of escaping to go riding by himself. Although Reagan was from the Midwest and I was from Boston, we both did a lot of early intense riding out on the dusty trails of the West, seeking solitude. It was dangerous to ride alone, but it was something we both took our chances with.

I joined the Secret Service in 1974. As it so often happens, the direction my life took hinged on two things: a telephone call from an old friend and one decision I made. I had returned to Boston after I graduated from the University of Arizona in the early 1970s. Tom McCarthy, also a former student from St. Clement, called me when I was back home. He was three years older than I was, and following his service as a U.S. Navy scuba diver in the

Vietnam War, he had become a Secret Service agent. "John, have you given any thought to the Secret Service?" he asked.

"No," I told him. "I had never even considered that."

"Well, why don't you at least talk to my boss, Stu Knight, who is the SAIC of the Boston field office?"

I called for an appointment, and after listening to Stu, I became quite interested. I wanted to become an agent. The Secret Service didn't recruit in those days. In fact, at that time there was only one job opening for every one hundred applicants. The background checks can take six months, and mine was taking awhile. At that point, I moved back to Arizona where I was just getting ready to enter the Arizona Highway Patrol training program. I then received word that I had made it over all the obstacles, and my security clearance had been okayed. They were ready for me to become an agent. I decided to join the Secret Service instead of becoming an Arizona Highway Patrol Officer.

When President Reagan was elected, he became the first modern president who enjoyed horseback riding, and I was the one tasked with establishing a Secret Service detail on horseback to protect him on his rides. The U.S. Park Police in Washington, D.C., put me through a three-month course in three weeks, which helped enormously. I requested that every Secret Service agent assigned to the horseback detail undergo similar training. The supervisor of the Secret Service was a little skeptical about it. He asked me, "Well, can't you just take someone that knows how to ride?" Secret Service agents are all Type A personalities who think they can ride. "Well, they need to prove to me they know how to ride," I told him.

The agents in training and I would run our horses through Rock Creek Park, a beautiful area with woodlands bordering

Washington, D.C. We'd ride wearing windbreakers that had the words Park Police on them, because we didn't want people to know we were Secret Service agents. It was dangerous, and several agents did get hurt. The rule was you couldn't go out alone. I insisted that we ride all day, and it got to the point where the officers were complaining. To them, riding was work, but to me, it was fun. Finally, they gave me permission to go out by myself, carrying a radio. During the weekends, people would be out picnicking in Rock Creek Park. They would offer me a hot dog and would want to pat the horse. I would let them, viewing it all as part of my public relations work.

It didn't take long for me to realize that I would have something special with President Reagan. You rarely encounter people like that in life: someone you know at first glance will become a true friend. I recalled seeing his movies as a kid and watching *General Electric Theater*. I was less familiar with him during the 1960s when he was governor of California. Growing up in Boston, California was like a foreign country to us. How could prim and proper Bostonians relate to the guys out on the West Coast with the tie-dyed shirts, shorts, and what we then called Jesus shoes—sandals? No one in Boston dressed like *that*. We thought the Beach Boys were from Venus and California was the land of fruits and nuts, but now Reagan and I were thrust together, and it didn't take long for us to begin to communicate in our own special way. As our friendship became stronger, we started to *really* understand each other. In fact, many times we never said anything, but we were still talking without saying a word.

Understandably, the communication between us at the White House was different from the talk at the ranch, and I always knew my place. I'd never speak to the President unless he spoke to me first. However, once he'd open that door, which he always did, we'd go at it. Regardless, I'd still be doing my job, and I had to be careful. Even though we shared a special friendship, I wasn't there to be his friend. Although it's good to be close and have your protectee trust you and know where you're coming from, becoming too close might cloud your judgment, and if something does happen, you might make a mistake. Because I was so close to him, I was overly concerned about that. Trouble was, you couldn't be around Reagan very long without becoming his friend.

We would seldom talk politics. There were times when the President just wanted to talk about something other than what was going on at the White House. I can vividly recall an exchange that we had just before the beginning of a head of state ceremony in 1983. I had just returned from my first year of riding with the Rancheros Visitadores, a men's riding group of which the President was also a member. We were having a south-ground arrival at the White House, which means that a U.S. president has invited the president of another country for an official visit. When the visiting president arrives, he receives an official welcome. Hundreds of people are let into the south grounds. A platform is set up, and the military band plays. Both leaders take their places on the platform where they each make a speech. After they are finished, they go into the White House and have tea or some other refreshment.

I happened to be at the post that day, which is the point where you walk through the set of doors from the Diplomatic Room out to the south grounds. I was standing post and along came the President with his military aide, his chief of staff, and a couple of cabinet members. As he was walking forward, the band received its cue to start playing "Hail to the Chief." The familiar don-don-da-don-don started to ring out, but when the President reached me, he stopped and asked, "John?"

"Mr. President?"

"How was Rancheros?"

"It was wonderful, sir."

"What did you do? Did you catch the pig?"

"Yes, I did."

Then he said, "I did the pig catching. You know, you grab them by their rear legs."

"I know that now, sir, cause I grabbed them by the front legs, and I had a very difficult time."

"No. You got to grab them by the back and you take them like pushing a wheelbarrow."

While we were having this conversation, you could still hear the military band outside playing. People were now starting to sweat, and so was I.

Still the President continued, "How was the horse? Did they give you a good horse? I talked to Trev Povah, president of Rancheros."

"Yeah. Trev took good care of me. Si Jenkins, owner of Jedlicka's Saddlery, got me a good horse and we had some great rides."

"Did you enter the rodeo?"

"Yes, sir."

"Did you do the hide race?"

"Yes, I did."

"Did you do the tie the ribbon on the calf's tail?"

"Yes, sir, I did," I answered, "but when the guy lassoed the calf, I put my hand on the rope which is a no-no. I didn't know it, and I thought I could pull that calf toward me. Well the rope went through my hand and just peeled all the skin right off."

The music continued to drone on outside, and now I was really starting to sweat. I looked at the chief of staff first. Then I turned and looked at the military aide. He needed to tell the President he had to go, because I was not going to tell him to.

Of course, the President had great respect for the visiting head of state. He just wanted to talk about the Rancheros. How many other people could he share this conversation with?

Judge Bill Clark, who was at first the President's national security advisor and later the secretary of the interior, was someone else I got to know through our love for riding during those White House days. He was also a member of Rancheros, and often he and I would ride U.S. Park Police horses together at Rock Creek Park.

After his meetings with the President, Judge Clark would come by and say, "Hi, John."

"Good morning, Mr. Secretary," I would answer.

Every time, he would put his hand up and say, "John, it's Bill."

"Not in the White House it isn't, sir," I would shoot back.

Our exchanges were always more formal at the White House than they were at the ranch, and they needed to be. The White House was the place where all the official business was taking place. When state dinners or other ceremonial events were held, the Secret Service agents would rotate from one position to another. I remember one black-tie function on the second floor. It was a dinner the President was hosting for a visiting president. Los Angeles Dodgers baseball manager, Tommy Lasorda, who was a good friend of the Reagans, was one of the guests, along with his date, Angie Dickinson. He had previously sent Dodgers baseball team warm-up jackets to the President and Mrs. Reagan. At the dinner, I noticed that while Mr. Lasorda was talking to one of the staff members, he kept looking over at me. I wondered what they were talking about.

Finally, he came over to me and said, "Agent Barletta, I'm Tommy Lasorda."

"I know who you are, sir."

"You ride with the President all the time, don't you?"

"That's one of my duties."

"Now, tell me the truth. Do they wear those jackets I sent them?"

"I'll tell you the truth. They're at Camp David. They wear them at Camp David when he goes riding or when they just go walking around."

"You ride with him all the time?"

"Yes, sir, I do."

The day after the dinner, there was a Dodger jacket waiting for me that had been delivered by Federal Express, and the next time we went to Camp David, I wore that jacket. At Camp David, the Secret Service command post called the Elm overlooks Aspen, the main cabin, which is where the President and the First Lady stay. The entire compound is secured by a United States Marine Corp detachment. When the President opens the front door, an alarm goes off to alert the agents that he is on his way out. It was a Saturday morning and the President and First Lady were going over to the building called the Laurel for his weekly radio broadcast. At once, I noticed that they were both in their Dodger jackets.

I happened to be in my Dodger jacket on that morning, too. My boss looked first at me and then at them, as we walked over to escort them. My boss asked, "John?"

"Boss, this was not planned," I answered. "This was not planned. I just wore the jacket."

When the President saw us he just smiled that Irish smile and winked, and Mrs. Reagan said, as she tugged on her own coat, "Nice jacket, John."

"Yes, ma'am."

WHENEVER WE got to the ranch, things were always a bit more relaxed. Still, I was mindful of the fact that he was the President and I was a Secret Service agent. I would always remember that. The Secret Service did all it could to make certain the President and First Lady still felt their ranch was a private place for them—a retreat. They installed the security in such a way that the Reagans would not hear or see all the mechanisms that had been put in place to protect them. Although the President knew it was all there, he would never complain that there were too many people around, as some other presidents have done.

One reason the ranch seemed worlds away from the White House is that while we were there, the President never talked to me about anything related to what was going on in Washington, D.C. Even though he shouldered some of the burdens of the world, he was always able to see and enjoy some of the great gifts of life. While riding, he would talk to me about the scenery. He'd say "This is what it's all about. Look at that tree. Look at those yellow poppy flowers. Those are the state flowers, John. That's Santa Rosa Island out there, John."

He was always looking for places along the path where he

needed to clear some brush. He would tell me to look at the bottom of the oak trees. "John, if I clear that up, the yellow poppies will thrive. They aren't growing because they can't get the sunlight. That's why Mother Nature allows fires, because they clean out the fields." After he cleaned out the bottom of the trees, everything did look healthier.

"John, see how the sunlight touches the trees," he'd say, "and notice how the mighty oak tree bends but doesn't break. Just hear that wind blow."

One time when we saw a gopher snake, he told me that he wanted them around. "There goes a gopher snake, John. You don't have the fellows kill them, do you?"

"No, sir," I reassured him.

"That's good, because they are good, friendly snakes that keep the gopher population under control. Now if there is a rattlesnake, well, that is a different story."

He loved being able to say what direction we were going. That was how I knew the ranch so well. At the beginning, I wouldn't know where we were or what direction we were facing. The President would say, "We're going to the northeast corner of the ranch, and when we get to that part, I want to go north."

"Is that right or left?" I would ask.

One of the first things the President noticed was that the other agents weren't as comfortable around the horses as I was. True horsemen relax around their horses. The President also appreciated that, like him, I rode English. There were always four agents, including me, on horses when the President went riding. The other three rode Western. The Secret Service gave me the authority to purchase four Western saddles from Si Jenkins.

They were Woffards—a good, basic leather saddle. With this type of saddle, they could carry gear with them. On an English saddle, you can't carry much gear. I didn't want to, because the agents around a president aren't going to stand and fight it out. If something did happen, we would've covered him with our bodies and evacuated. We'd practice and practice that repeatedly.

Another thing the President liked was the way I tied horses. Everybody has a way of tying, and I use a slipknot. To tie this knot, you take the lead rope and you put it over the hitching post. You then bring the lead rope underneath the hitching post. Next you take your right hand, grasp the bottom lead rope knuckles up, and then with the lead rope in hand, you rotate it until your knuckles are facing the ground. Finally, you take the tip of the lead rope and twist it and pull it through until it tightens. If there is a problem, the horse *usually* can't get out of it, and if you tie the knot properly, all you have to do to release the horse is pull on it.

There is one thing you never do: tie a horse by the reins, which certain people did up at the ranch. You just don't do that. I can recall the time one of the military aides wrapped his reins around the hitching post. I'm not picking on the military aides, because some of them have been my fast, longtime friends, but every good horseman knows that you never tie a horse by the reins. Anyway, when this happened, the President looked at the reins and then he looked at me, never saying a word. I walked over, undid the reins, and put the halter lead rope on the hitching post the way it was supposed to be. He just gave me a nod and a smile. The military aide acted like, *what's going on?* but not a word was said.

Besides the First Lady, no one else at the ranch had ridden with him before. One time some friends came up, the Jorgensons, and they rode with him, but that never happened again. He almost always had ridden alone, but now he had me, and he liked that. I once tried to get Dennis Le Blanc to go riding. He was the California State Police Officer who had been on Reagan's protective detail while he was governor, and he was at the White House for a while. He always came to the ranch to cut wood with the President. I said, "Dennis, why don't you ride with us? I'll tack up a horse for you."

"No, John, no. I chop wood with him. I don't ride horses with him."

In the beginning, the President and I would ride for two or two-and-a-half hours and sometimes twice a day when we were at the ranch. At Camp David, we would go twice a day for the same length of time. Unfortunately, that became too time consuming for him. He had work to do, but at the ranch, most of his official business was "homework," so that left him more time to ride.

3

The Rider and His Ranch

Reagan called it his open cathedral in the sky: majestic hills rising out of the dusty ground high above the Santa Ynez Valley, strong and beautiful oak trees with twisted trunks overlooking incredible vistas of the Pacific Ocean, and rugged backcountry with endless trails. Though his humble ranch was far from majestic, the natural beauty visible from the 2,250-foot-high mountaintop made him feel like he was on top of the world.

As he often put it, "Rancho del Cielo can make you feel as if you are on a cloud." It was simple and comfortable, embodying the character of a leader who has become a hero to many. The principles he esteemed were constant throughout his life—hope, simplicity, hard work, and optimism—and he walked and rode Rancho del Cielo with those same guiding values.

The Reagans purchased the ranch in November 1974. The name of the property at the time was Tip Top Ranch. That would never work. This place on the side of the mountain was so much more to them than that. They renamed their new property

Rancho del Cielo (Spanish for "Ranch in the Sky"). Twenty-nine miles northwest of Santa Barbara, it was their escape from Washington, D.C., from their aides, and from the many people constantly tugging at them. In all my years in the Secret Service, I never really heard the President complain about his schedule, but there was one exception. Every once in a while, he would turn to his chief of staff, Michael Deaver, and say, "Mike, the schedule looks fine, but I don't see any ranch time in here. I don't see a ranch trip in the schedule."

Like all other presidents, he still had to carry the weighty burdens of that office with him, but at least at the ranch, he was in the place where he felt most comfortable. While riding his horse on the endless trails of his 688 acres, he could be alone with his thoughts and nature. When we were at the White House, I'd be on post, and he'd come by and say to me while grabbing and shaking his lapel, "Well, John, in four days we can get out of these clothes, get in some boots and jeans, and we'll be riding."

For most of his adult life, Reagan owned a ranch somewhere in California. From his childhood days on, Reagan had looked to nature for solace and strength, and he would retreat to the wonderment of the outdoors whenever he needed to sort things out and make decisions.

None of his ranches were palatial. They were always like him—simple, rugged, and sturdy. When people first got a glimpse of Rancho del Cielo, they were surprised. When the last president of the Soviet Union, Mikhail Gorbachev, saw the tiny adobe home in 1992, I could see how stunned he was. Of course, the point was Reagan bought the place *because* it was simple. On the wall of his small adobe home, the President had a plaque he prized greatly, with a quote from Horatio's *The Bridge*: "How can a man die better than facing fearful odds for the ashes of his fathers and the temples of his gods?"

He had purchased his first ranch years before he met Nancy. It was a small eight-acre ranch near Northridge in the lush San Fernando Valley. He kept a few horses there and would escape to it on weekends when he wasn't shooting a film. While most of his friends were spending their weekends chasing starlets at the Brown Derby in Hollywood, Reagan was at the ranch, riding horses, fixing fences, and cleaning out the stalls.

His second ranch was a 290-acre property in Malibu Canyon named Yearling Row, which he purchased in 1951. It was in Cornell Corners right by Malibu Lake, and there he was able to truly build something. He raised thoroughbreds and had two brood mares named Torch Carrier and Bracing. Every year, he would produce two foals from those two mares, and each year, a guy would come by to decide if the foals were good enough for the Delmar sale, the premier horse sale on the West Coast. Reagan's foals were always of quality and always made the sale. The shingled house was small and modest. Mrs. Reagan was afraid it was a firetrap, and they never stayed there for the night. On the walls inside, though, they had hung pictures from their various motion pictures. Reagan just loved the place, and he would work his heart out fixing it. He built sturdy wooden stalls, marked out the trails, and erected a new fence. He loved working with his hands, and Mrs. Reagan would sometimes join him in his labors by painting fence posts or helping to clean things up. There were three-and-a-half miles of a three-rail aluminized fence on that place, and Mrs. Reagan followed behind her husband, helping to paint the fence after he put it up. They did the whole thing by themselves.

There were two reservoirs on the property. Above one of the reservoirs was a road called Mulholland Drive. One day, a car with a fancy government seal on it pulled up to the side of the road. The driver got out and looked down at the place. Finally he drove in and asked Reagan, "Are you the owner?"

"Yes, I am," he answered.

"Did you build these reservoirs?"

"Yes, I did."

"Well, you know, you're entitled to a government subsidy for all this. Fill out these applications."

Reagan interrupted him, "You know, when I built them, I built them with my own funds, and I never intended to have any government subsidy. I'd like to keep it that way."

In the late 1950s, there was a fire called the Liberty Fire that started in nearby Liberty Canyon. It burned through Yearling Row and took out the main barn, but not the stables. In fact, the stables are still there.

At lunchtime, the work hands at the ranch would sit around in a circle and eat together. Reagan would just bring something like an apple and a peanut butter and jelly sandwich—nothing formal. A friend of Reagan's during those years told me that at lunch one day Reagan said, "You know, the Air Force just junked or salvaged five million dollars' worth of dark glasses, and the Navy just ordered the same thing for another five million dollars. It just drives me nuts. You know, I ought to become president of the United States."

According to Reagan's friend, the foreman was the only one who stayed on the place. Reagan would say, "Well, I won't be around for a while, I've got to go to work." That meant he was going to get on a train and go back East for his speeches with

General Electric. He held that property for almost twenty years, finally selling it to his neighbor, Paramount Pictures, when he became governor.

In 1968, the Reagans purchased Rancho California in Riverside County, north of San Diego. It was remote and far off the beaten trail, and Reagan's hope was to turn this ranch into a retreat. In Sacramento, he no doubt felt confined, and this was the place that would allow him to get out and do some riding once he left office. However, he became frustrated, because there was no water or power service. So he decided to sell the place and began his search for the perfect place on earth. That search eventually led to his ranch in the sky.

Longtime friend Bill Wilson was the one who found the Reagans their final ranch. Wilson and his wife Betty had a ranch near the base of Refugio Canyon north of Santa Barbara, and the Reagans visited them often. During those visits Reagan really grew to like the area, and so when Bill heard there was a ranch for sale, he contacted Reagan at once. After he was elected president, Reagan appointed Bill as ambassador to the Vatican.

Reagan didn't need any urging. Soon after, Bill drove with the Reagans up the Refugio Canyon Road to see the place. The drive up the winding, one-lane road is seven miles long, and it seems to go on and on. Mrs. Reagan asked, "Where *are* you taking us?" They just kept going, with no answer.

Finally, even Reagan said, "Bill, is this going to end at some point?" It was soon apparent that the drive up the tortuous road was well worth it. Even before they arrived, Reagan was awed by the graceful mountains and thick clusters of oaks. "It's absolutely gorgeous here," he told Bill. "I love it." Once they reached the ranch, the Reagans decided almost immediately that they would buy this place.

Rancho del Cielo is the only one in the Santa Ynez Mountain Range that is shaped like a dish and thereby provides some great useable land. When Reagan first bought the property, it was much sparser than it is now. There was nothing on the ranch, just the simple adobe house built a century earlier, though "house" might be too kind a word. It was more like a hut, with aluminum sheets for the roof. There was no pond, few trees by the house, and no fences. Reagan, however, looked at that plot of land the way he looked at everything: there is an opportunity here.

He went to work at once. By himself, the President laid the sandstone patio in front of the house. He would go out with his Jeep and collect large sandstone rocks and bring them back. Next, he would pour the concrete before laying the rocks in place. He was very handy.

The President extended the house. Previously, it had ended where the L-shaped living room-dining room was. He took down the chicken wire and the corrugated aluminum. He said, "This house needs to go back to looking the way nature wanted it to, to fit in here on this beautiful spot. No aluminum. We'll get rid of *all* of that."

He also erected the fence, largely by himself. In the hot sun, he would use a two-handed posthole digger and pull out clumps of earth from the rock-hard soil. Next, he would gently lay in the telephone poles that Dennis had brought up from Pacific Gas and Electric, lining them up. There is a short video of him in which you see him dressed in a tee shirt and work gloves digging

the holes for the telephone poles. He was using a string to measure to see if they were even. Looking at the camera, he said,
"Very scientific work."

He loved physical labor, which was something the press
could never quite understand. Every year, the President hosted a
party for the traveling press at Barney Clinger's estate in Santa
Barbara. At that party, Sam Donaldson once said, "Now, Mr.
President, I hear you like to go out and trim trees and cut wood."

"Yes, yes I do," the President responded

Donaldson went on, "Now, just how big is the ranch?"

"Six hundred and eighty-eight acres."

"Well, Mr. President, at that rate you'll never be through
trimming."

"I hope not, Sam," he said.

The press was allowed to come to the ranch for just a few
events during Reagan's entire presidency. One was during the
Queen's visit and another was when he signed the tax relief bill,
which was the largest tax cut in American history. Back in 1981,
there had been a spirited debate on Capitol Hill before the
Democratic Congress finally passed the President's tax cut. He
chose to sign the bill at the ranch where he was riding, rather
than return to the White House. In the photos of him signing
the bill, he is sitting on one of the pigskin-covered chairs at the
table on the patio he built.

While he was signing the tax bill, Sam Donaldson blurted
out, "Mr. President, are you thinking about selling this ranch
anytime soon?"

The President shot back, "You can't sell heaven."

Another time, at a birthday party for Mrs. Reagan, the

President said that if the ranch wasn't heaven, it "probably has the same zip code."

A RANCH IS more than a house and fence posts. Besides providing a home for the Reagans, Rancho del Cielo also accommodated many wild animals. When I first arrived there in November 1980, there were bears, bobcats, mountain lions, rattlesnakes, and gopher snakes. When we were out riding, there were a few special places we'd venture to at times. One of those spots was Snake Lake, a small isolated lake just off the property, which I don't think anyone ever rode to except us. The dirt road to the lake is now overgrown with heavy brush, so you can no longer get down there. On some of our early rides together, the President and I would ride down there and we'd see huge bear prints. The bears would walk out into the middle of the lake, plop down, and lick the water. That sure seemed strange to me but I guess not to them. Soon after the new presidential staff invaded, however, some of the animals moved away. They left once we started to erect temporary housing, dig the well, and fly the helicopters in and out. It became too noisy for them.

Still, there was plenty of wildlife around. One morning, there were four gopher snakes outside the President's front door, just off to the left in the grass. Nonpoisonous, they can get to at least six feet long. Unless they are provoked, they will not normally bite a human. The snakes that morning were mating in a big ball, and the President found that fascinating. Leaning over with his hands on hips, he got really close. About that time, Mrs. Reagan emerged from the house and pleaded, "John, can you get him away from them?"

"Mr. President," I said, "we should back away."

Nevertheless he wouldn't move. "Gopher snakes won't hurt you."

Another time when we were out for a ride, we saw a bobcat and her three young cubs. They walked right across the trail we were riding on.

One day when we were coming in from a ride, we saw a hawk soaring and circling. The President pointed it out. "John, that hawk sees something." When we got to a clearing where we could see the ground, the hawk folded it wings and dove. It grabbed a huge gopher snake with its talons and then started flapping its wings so it could carry the snake off, but the snake was about five feet long and was really wiggling. The hawk tried to fly away with the snake, but soon dropped it because it was just too heavy for him to lift, giving the snake his chance to slither away.

For the agents, an occasional rattlesnake and the dangers of riding a horse weren't the only challenges at the ranch. Getting there could be tricky. The winding road was nearly impossible for Reagan's limo, and the drivers had a heck of a time making that large vehicle take those hairpin turns. Besides the narrow road through the canyon and up the mountain, the only other way to get to the ranch was by helicopter. While Reagan was still the president-elect, he rode up like the rest of us, though he never minded. He wasn't given a military helicopter yet. Once president, however, he arrived on *Marine One* every time except once during his presidency. Still, the members of the presidential entourage had to travel up that treacherous one-lane road. That was the worst part of the job. Three shifts a day would go up that road in Chevy Suburbans. The strain on the vehicles was so great that every ten thousand miles the tires and brakes had to be replaced.

After he left the White House, the President always looked forward to the drive up the winding road. Mrs. Reagan would fall asleep just about every time, but not him. He would just stare out the window, enjoying nature. From the second he left his house, he would time the drive, and when we got out of the car he would say, "Well, you've got the record time for getting me here." Of course, then the guys driving started to compete with one another to see who could get him to the ranch the fastest.

The ride from the President's Bel Air residence to the ranch has sixty-five-mile-an-hour speed limits, and it would be very embarrassing if the California Highway Patrol stopped us. "Guys," I said, "we do sixty-five miles an hour!"

Members of Reagan's Secret Service protective detail loved going to the ranch. It was an opportunity for us to get out of our suits and bulletproof vests and put on our jeans, boots, T-shirts, and baseball caps. However, I still insisted on some decorum, and I had to get creative to find a way to conceal our weapons. Most agents have their weapons on their right hips, and vests that always conceal them. The vests also conceal their radios. For me, it worked to have my radio on my left hip, the wires running underneath my shirt up into my right ear. I said, "You guys all go down and buy those sleeveless denim vests." I suggested Jedlicka's, the local Western shop in Santa Barbara owned by my friend Si Jenkins, where I had purchased many of the riding supplies for the President and the Secret Service. In no way did I want the President and First Lady to see reminders that, even though private, this was a dangerous situation. There was no need to do that. Everybody agreed to my request.

From a security standpoint, the ranch was a double-edged sword. It was so remote that most people didn't even know where it was. If I gave someone the address, they wouldn't be able to find it. That was good. There was incredibly thick brush all around. No one could drive up there or could come up the side of the mountain. You could only drive the main road, and that was always secure. We also had the FAA put out a P52 Notices to Airmen (NOTAMS) stating to aircraft that they were in restricted airspace and could not go below two hundred feet over the ranch. Once, a pilot violated the P52, flying just yards above the helicopter landing. He was arrested and lost his pilot's license.

The FAA runs a VORTAC (short for VHF omnidirectional range/tactical aircraft control) up on the highest spot on the ranch. A VORTAC is like a road sign. Pilots flying overhead home in on that VORTAC, and from that they receive all the directions and then proceed to their destinations. We went to the FAA to see if the VORTAC could be moved. They said they could move it but then started to explain just what it would take. They told us that the nuclear submarines use it to triangulate location, and when Vandenberg Air Force Base launches their missiles and rockets, they go by that VORTAC signal. The list of uses for that VORTAC went on and on until finally we said we did not want to cause all those disruptions. The government ended up paying the President to have that VORTAC on his land. That mountain range is one of the best for it, and years earlier, before he was president, when they had wanted to put it up he had said okay. Still, to this day, it is a very important piece of machinery. They come up there all the time to fine-tune it.

Our biggest security concern was the President's daily horse riding, which presented all sorts of challenges. We had to make sure that the rugged area was secure and that there were no physical hazards that could harm the President. Then there was also the matter of the horses themselves. Where they in good shape? How were their temperaments? The President was determined that not only he and Mrs. Reagan would have a good time but we all would. He wanted to make sure we were all enjoying ourselves while on the job.

He would usually come up for his rides like clockwork at nine a.m. and would return in time for lunch at noon. In the early days, he would sometimes also ride in the afternoon. Before a ride, we would study the big detailed map on the wall in the tack barn and carefully devise where we were going to ride that day. Wanting my input, he'd ask, "Well, what if we go here, and then if we go left we'll be over where that tree is, and then, after that, what if we go there?"

I always answered, "Mr. President, that's fine with me."

"You sure?"

"Yes, sir."

"Well, maybe we can go—"

"Sir, you can do whatever you want. When we reach where you want to go, and if you want to change the route, I can change my men around. Don't worry about it. Whatever you—"

Then he would say, "I want the fellows to have a good ride too." He was so nice and enthusiastic about everything.

"Sir, we're not here to have a good time."

He'd look at me and say, "Though we are having a good time."

"You're the one, sir, who must enjoy this. You do what you like, and we'll be able to stay right with you."

However, that never would satisfy him, and he persisted, "No, I want you to have a good ride also."

Finally I would say, "I'll have a good ride no matter where you go, because I'm on a horse." It was then he would stop talking and just smile, because that was exactly how he felt too, and he liked that.

He would show Mrs. Reagan the map. "Now we're going to go over here. John says we can go there."

She'd look over at me, not having a clue how to read that map. All she would say was, "Oh, that sounds like a good route, honey." Then she would look at me again and shrug her shoulders. I would just laugh.

While Reagan loved the outdoors, he didn't like the things that people usually associate with it—hunting and fishing. He liked target shooting, but I don't recall him ever talking about hunting. I asked him about it once, and he just said, "No." It just didn't interest him.

He felt the same way about fishing. I only saw him fish one time from a private boat during a trip to Alaska. He caught a halibut. Catching a halibut in Alaska is like pulling up a rock. They feed off the bottom. The one the President hooked weighed twenty pounds, but they can go all the way up to sixty pounds and above. Once hooked, you crank and crank the line because they don't fight. It tasted wonderful, but to him it didn't mean that much. While he liked boats, he never was around one except for that trip.

Besides riding horses, the President relaxed chopping wood and clearing brush. He loved to take out the chain saw, and there'd be wood chips flying everywhere. Dennis LeBlanc and Barney Barnett, a California Highway Patrol Officer who was also Reagan's driver when he was governor, would help the President at the ranch. In fact, every time the President went to the ranch, Barney and Dennis would stay there with him, and they would chop wood together. They had their own quarters in a small trailer. Barney always called the President "Governor," because of his earlier days with him as his driver. For sentimental reasons, Barney still called him "Governor" after Reagan was elected president. Only Barney could do that. Dennis, always levelheaded, later went to work at the White House for the military office in the East Wing. After he left Washington, D.C., he still kept going to the ranch whenever the President wanted him to.

Barney and Dennis would be working with him, and it sounded like the attack of the killer bees, because two or three chain saws would be going at one time. The toughest thing Reagan did was use his pole saw to cut tree limbs high up. The pole saw is for reaching up and cutting maybe one- or two-inch limbs, but he'd take down a six-inch limb, which is physically demanding. You're basically cutting wood while holding your hands over your head. Unless you're in great condition, you won't be able to raise your arms the next day, but he didn't even break a sweat. It was strange. Barney and Dennis, who were working with him, would have their shirts soaked through with sweat, but not the President.

Occasionally, I would catch him trying to tackle something I just didn't think he should be doing. I'd rush over to Dennis and talk it over with him. Dennis would say, "That's way too big, Mr. President. Maybe I should try that." Dennis always had the chain saw, and before the President could answer, Dennis would have the limb cut down. If we didn't handle it that way, the President would have worked on it for too long.

The work really helped him relax, and often he didn't want to take a break. I would ask, "Mr. President, do you want some water?"

"No," he would answer still cutting away.

I would then walk over to Dennis and say, "You know, it's ninety-five degrees out. Do me a favor, go over and tell him you're taking a break. If you tell him you need a break, then he'll stop too."

"Sir, why don't we take a break?" Dennis would ask him.

"Well, I'm okay."

Well, I'm not," Dennis would tell him. "I need a break. I need some water."

"Okay." The President would carefully put the pole saw down and walk over to the Jeep where he'd drink some water and usually tell a story. There wouldn't be any sweat on his face. The only time he'd stop working would be when someone else wanted to take a break. He was too polite to say no.

The ranch house didn't have air-conditioning or heating, but it had two fireplaces. In the wintertime, if it fell below eighty degrees, Mrs. Reagan would be cold. She needed a sweater. Since the President had cut enough wood to heat New York City, both of those fireplaces would be literally raging all the time.

The President would split the wood to fit into the fireplace and then stack it. Although he liked using an axe, he used the automatic splitter because cutting it with the axe took forever. Dennis came up with the idea of the splitter. You put the log in the holder, you press a button, and it rips the piece of wood in two. It is a very dangerous machine. One time Dennis had an accident and lost the tip of his finger. The chipper, however, is the most dangerous machine of all. If you throw brush and wood in there and a piece of branch catches on your jeans, it will pull you right in and there will be nothing left of you. That used to scare the hell out of me. Sometimes the President would be attempting to throw brush and wood in there, and I would say, "Dennis, *please* don't let him do that. It's too dangerous. I can't stand this anymore. I can't stand watching it."

"Mr. President," Dennis would ask him diplomatically, "why don't you drag the brush to this point, and then I'll put it into the chipper?"

"Well, all right," he would agree. He just wouldn't say no, and we counted on that. It was a relief.

THE RANCH was really just the President and First Lady's place. Their family rarely came there. I think their daughter Patti rode just once at the ranch. The rest of the family came up for Mrs. Reagan's birthday, but that was it. Aides and advisors rarely came. Even visits by the chief of staff and members of the cabinet were few. The only time the President's staff was present was for his Saturday half-hour radio broadcast.

Nobody but the Reagans actually slept at the ranch. The agents had three shifts and stayed down in hotels in Santa

Barbara, and the staff stayed in hotels too. Everyone loved it, including the press. They would go to the beach sometimes and play volleyball, having a great time while the President was working on the ranch. The White House press office would give the media a rundown of what Reagan had done that day: well, he rode his horse and chopped wood and that was the end of it. The normal routine seldom changed. Sam Donaldson would be on the beach, and he would put his jacket, shirt, and tie on but still be in his shorts. They would film him from the waist up. He would say, "President Reagan did this today. This is Sam Donaldson with the President in Santa Barbara."

"You aren't with the President," I would tell him. "You aren't even near the President." Everybody from the area loved the President's staff and treated them like gold.

Each president can designate one other place other than the White House as a residence. That's what justifies that residence being secured by Secret Service. In contrast to President George H. W. Bush's compound in Kennebunkport, Maine, or President Clinton's vacation wanderings, the Reagans' ranch really was a place of solitude. The President chose the ranch, not their other home, as their residence. He said, "That's it, no question." He sold the Pacific Palisades house. The ranch was everything to him.

Most people called the ranch the Western White House. The Reagans, however, never called it that. Yet, wherever the president goes, the White House moves with him. The presidency always goes with the president. There is a special military unit called the White House Communications Agency (WHCA) that always travels with him. The members of this unit wear civilian attire, and WHCA is the focal point for all the incoming and outgoing calls.

Much of what the president does at the White House can be done wherever he is—even on the back of a horse. If there is a major problem, a president likes to have his cabinet around, but rarely is the cabinet all in Washington, D.C., at the same time anyway. I just think most people feel more comfortable when they see a president at the White House—they think that he needs to be there to be in control. Just think of what the reaction would have been if Russia had been in turmoil and the President had been out riding his horse. While it may have appeared bad, it really would not have meant that he did not have things under control. He could have just picked up the satellite phone, which he often did.

Occasionally, the rhythm at the ranch would be disrupted by world events. In September 1983, the President received a call from his national security advisor, Judge Bill Clark, while he was out riding. A military aide alerted me and said the President had to take a call. We knew it was something serious. "Mr. President, they are telling me that you have to take an emergency phone call," I told him.

"Okay," he said calmly. "How are we going to do it?"

"Sir, we will ride back to the White House Communications Agency." It was located in a Chevy Suburban, with lots of antennas protruding from the roof, equipped with special devices to meet all the President's communication needs. In it was the phone the President could use to call anyone in the world. Even when riding, this vehicle was close behind. The President rode back to the WHCA vehicle at once and took the call from Bill

Clark. He was told that the Russians had just shot down KAL-007, a civilian 747 airliner, killing all the passengers aboard.

There were only two times I saw him angry, and that was one of them. When we resumed our ride, he pounded on his saddle and said, "Those were innocent people, those damned Russians. They knew that was a civilian aircraft." He was visibly upset. That was one of the few times we left the ranch early.

To President Reagan, his ranch was what American life was all about. What could be better than someone riding a horse through the open land that he owned? That picture was the epitome of America.

I believe deep down he embraced the cowboy ideals of the West, such as a firm handshake and friendship. The history of the West is one of hardworking cowboys, the John Wayne types, and he truly believed in hard work. Let's just all chip in and get it done, it doesn't matter who gets the credit. That was Reagan's way. In doing business, all that was needed was a firm handshake. A cowboy would die before he'd break his word. His word was his bond. (Today you hire six lawyers to break your word for you.) Cowboys always told the direct truth and were never out of control. When you think of a cowboy, the myth of a cowboy, you think of a man who is hardworking, good to his animals, and takes care of his equipment. He never starts a conflict but will finish one if he needs to.

No matter what your politics were, if you sat down with the President and talked to him, he would have some answers for you. You might not have liked his answers or his way of thinking to solve your problem, but he always had a solution. If you didn't agree with his solutions, that was okay too. Everyone was

entitled to his or her opinion. The President's philosophy of a
firm handshake spilled over into the way he handled politics. If
you examine his history with Gorbachev, he viewed him not only
as someone he might like to work with but as someone he *needed*
to cooperate with. He figured Gorbachev was somebody he
could deal with, so he was going to give him his word and stick
to it. He was extremely anxious to meet the new Soviet premier.
That was one case where he did not rely as much on his advisors
who were recommending a different approach with Gorbachev.

Obviously, there were clear differences between the President and Gorbachev. One time, he wrote a letter to the Soviet
leader using some pretty strong words about communism and
nonbelief in God. He told Gorbachev that he should let his
people go to church if they wanted to. The State Department did
not want him to send that letter. They felt it was a slap in the
face to the Russians. Although he never said anything harsh to
them, they would argue. Finally the President said, "You send
your letters, and I'll send mine." In other words, this conversation is over, and that's what I'm going to do. They knew not to
push him one more step.

Then there was the evil empire speech. On *Air Force One*,
his advisors kept telling him he couldn't say that. They would
cross it off the speech and then hand it back to him. He'd immediately write it back in. They'd cross it off. He'd write it back
in. After about the third time, he said, "Listen. You can cross this
off all you want, but that's what I'm going to say." They were
all left just wringing their hands.

I was often struck by how President Reagan interacted with
Gorbachev. Before he met with him at the summit in Reykjavik,
Iceland, the President spoke to the interpreter and asked that

when he interpreted Gorbachev's words, he wanted him to translate not just the words, but the feelings behind them. The feelings were important to him; whether Gorbachev was being
sincere and honest. You can say, "It's a nice day" and not really
mean it, or you can say, "It's a *nice* day out!" exuding enthusiasm.
The interpreter did that for him. Never before had I heard
anyone request to have an interpreter translate the emotions of
what was being said.

WHILE WE ALL KNOW Ronald Reagan as a public figure, he was
in many respects a very private man, who enjoyed solitude and
being alone. He spent most of his childhood in crowded neigh-
borhoods and rented apartments and houses, playing on porches
or in yards. There certainly weren't horses around. I think that
was why he cherished his ranches so much, because he finally
was able to have them. Even as a little boy, though, he found
places to escape to, to be alone. In one of the rented homes he
lived in, he discovered a collection of birds' eggs and butterflies
in the attic that had been left by the previous tenant. These fas-
cinated him. The other place he'd steal to was the Rock River in
Dixon, Illinois, where he would go for long walks. Here was the
open space he longed for.

Growing up, the sport he enjoyed most was swimming,
another solitary activity. He was a lifeguard at Rock River, a
challenging branch of the Mississippi. That river was swift, and
for people who weren't used to it, it was dangerous. Often, both
young kids and older people needed help. It has been said that
Reagan saved seventy-seven people, making a notch on a log
every time he did. While I found that hard to believe, that
number has been documented.

He truly loved being an actor, and later he became an extremely well-versed orator, speaking in front of thousands of people. Yet, the actual idea of being a celebrity or public figure was not that important to him. He most enjoyed being alone in a quiet place like the ranch.

Reagan had a fascination with creation and what he called "the handiwork of God." He had a deep and abiding belief in God and was a profoundly spiritual person. The President and Billy Graham were great friends, and they would talk about their faith.

When we were out riding, he would sometimes quote the Bible and talk to me about it. Those were heavy, but usually one-sided, conversations between us. He truly believed that God worked through history. I would just respond, "Uh-huh. Yes, sir." I just have never been a deep thinker about thoughts like that.

At the ranch, more than anywhere else, the President could enjoy all of God's marvelous creation. He would say, "Only God could put this together. Man cannot do this. Every leaf, every tree, that sky, those mountains, that ocean." He would thoughtfully point to each thing while he was talking. Standing under the huge sky, he felt as if he had everything he needed right there.

He saw a natural order to things, an order designed by the Creator. "This is God's plan," he would say about the rhythm of nature. "It's not man's plan."

Once, someone tried to trip him up and said, "Well, if God wanted the brush cleared, He would have done so."

Always ready with a quick response, he said, "Well, no, that's not a good argument. That's not true. God gave man a free will."

That was how he viewed life and history. Man could take

part, try to intervene, and make decisions that could have an impact. Beyond man's choices, however, God had his plan. He'd talk so calmly about God. He truly believed that after the assassination attempt, God had a plan for him. He said, "God thought— Well God doesn't think, God knew that I needed a nudge. God wanted that assassination attempt to happen. He gave me a wake-up call. Everything I do from now on, I owe to God. He wanted everything to happen to me—except what you did to my suit." He complained for years that we had cut off his brand new suit to save his life. He had worn it only once.

4

A Strong Man
and His Horses

Reagan was thoroughly grateful to his horses for allowing him to ride them—for giving him a better view of nature. We'd be riding together in a vehicle, and he'd say, "It sure will be nice to be on a horse soon. You are higher up, and you can see everything better. There's a huge difference between that and driving around in a Jeep."

Reagan liked thoroughbreds, which are typically tall and lean with long legs and long necks. He rode true athletic horses, the kind only an experienced rider can usually control, since they can be a bit hard to handle. A good quarter horse, which is a stout, thick-bodied animal, can be very forgiving when you make a mistake. However, if you make a mistake with most thoroughbreds, there is not too much forgiveness in them. You had better be sitting deep in the saddle.

That was the case particularly with the President's favorite horse, El Alamein. He was a powerful and difficult horse to ride. El Alamein was sixteen hands high (meaning sixteen human hands, measuring each hand with the four fingers together) and in very good shape. Most people associate President Reagan with a white horse. However, in the horse world, El Alamein was known as a gray. There are very few truly white horses. They are albinos with pink eyes and pink muzzles, and they do not get along with the elements. Few of them make it as working horses.

A lesser rider could never have handled El Alamein, but the President liked riding him because it was a challenge. El Alamein was an Arabian thoroughbred mix, which is called an Anglo Arab. When considering a horse's temperament, an Arabian thoroughbred is probably the worst combination you can have. They have incredible staying power, and they will just keep going. At the same time, they are flighty horses and are prone to unpredictable behavior. While they usually are small, sometimes when you mix an Arabian with a thoroughbred, you can get a sixteen-hands-high horse like El Alamein.

El Alamein was an unbelievably strong horse. Dr. Doug Herthel, a prominent veterinarian in the Santa Ynez Valley who owns and runs the Alamo Pintado Equine Clinic, cared for the President's horses. He would put El Alamein on the treadmill in his clinic to show me just how strong he was. Few veterinarians have treadmills in their offices, but Dr. Herthel's clinic is considered one of the best in the world. He often puts racehorses on the treadmill to check out their relative health. El Alamein would go from a resting respiratory level to the desired level in two minutes while it took other thoroughbreds five minutes to reach the same point. While those thoroughbreds were in great shape, El Alamein was even stronger.

Keeping El Alamein checked up—in control—was very important. He was flighty and always eager to run. On several different occasions when I rode him, I felt that there might be something wrong with him. Finally, I asked Dr. Herthel to come up to the ranch to take El Alamein for a ride and to get his expert opinion. We had been out riding for more than twenty minutes, and Dr. Herthel, a seasoned rider himself, hadn't said a word. I did notice that he was having a little trouble controlling El Alamein, so I finally asked, "Well, Doug, what do you think? Do you feel that there is anything wrong with him?"

"No, I don't feel anything wrong with him, but I can't believe you let the president of the United States ride this dingbat."

Still, President Reagan loved that horse. He had received him as a gift from President Portillo of Mexico in 1980. Portillo had El Alamein trained so that when he came out of his stall he would rear up and walk on his hind legs. Regardless of whether you know horses or not, that is going to impress you. Portillo gave the horse to Reagan, I'm sure, as a gesture of friendship.

The President rode El Alamein for about ten years. It was almost as if this strong man and this strong horse really understood each other. When it was time to find the President a new horse, I acquired a big, strong quarter horse for him through Dr. Herthel. This horse, however, had a much better personality. I took him up to the ranch and showed him to the President. He rode him and liked him at once. He then wanted to know what I thought. "Mr. President, I think he's a damn good horse."

"How much will the horse cost?" he asked.

"Doug Herthel will give him to you if you like him."

"No, no I want to pay him for him," the President insisted. So I gave him a figure. Thoughtfully considering the number I had given him, he asked me, "Would that be fair? Is the horse worth that?"

"The horse is worth double that. That would be a fair price for Doug." He immediately sat down and wrote the check.

"I'm going to call him Sergeant Murphy," he announced, naming him after one of his motion pictures filmed in 1937. The President rode Sergeant Murphy for six years, and another bond between the rider and his horse was established.

Gimcrack, a dark bay thoroughbred, was also a favorite of the President. Gimcrack belonged to the U.S. Park Police and was a seventeen-hands-high horse, weighing in at thirteen hundred pounds. That thoroughbred moved like a cat. He had been used for foxhunting in Middleburg, Virginia, and the owners donated him to the U.S. Park Police. The first time I rode Gimcrack was in 1983 when I was with Dennis Ayers. He was the sergeant in charge of the U.S. Park Police training barn located in Rock Creek Park in Washington, D.C., under the bridge near Georgetown. The training barn held thirty horses for the use of the Park Police officers who patrolled the area, mostly for security purposes and demonstrations.

I met Dennis at the barn and he introduced me to Gimcrack.

Dennis got on his horse, and I mounted Gimcrack to see what he was like. We rode through Rock Creek on a dirt path down by the C and O Canal along the Potomac River. Reacting to something he saw, Gimcrack shied away, spinning in a 180-degree turn. I gathered up the reins, and he held. I turned to Dennis and said, "I think the President will love this horse. He moves like a cat." The President did end up liking Gimcrack, and he rode him at Camp David often. Still, even for the most skillful horsemen, riding these horses can sometimes lead to disaster—or at least near disaster. Unfortunately, Gimcrack was no exception.

The President had made a practice early on in his administration of saluting back to the Marine sentries who saluted him. He did it to the sentries at the base of the stairs when we arrived or departed on *Marine One* or *Air Force One* and again to the sentries at Camp David. The Marine Corps is charged with the security of *Marine One*, while the Air Force is responsible for the security of *Air Force One*. When the President isn't on *Marine One*, it's not *Marine One* anymore, but it's always secured.

Anytime the President, staff, and agents board or disembark *Marine One*, there is always a Marine in dress blues at the bottom of the stairs. When the President comes on board, the Marine sentry salutes and holds his salute until the President gets in. Then when the President comes down the stairs of his helicopter or plane, a sentry again salutes smartly until the President walks by.

Saluting was not something that presidents had done before. President Reagan was the first one to do it. In fact, even though President Eisenhower was a general, he never saluted. In June 1983, we were at the Marine Barracks in Washington, D.C., for the swearing-in ceremony of Marine General P. X. Kelly as the new commandant of the Marine Corp. As the President was walking past the rows of Marines, he asked General Kelly if it was okay to salute the troops back when they saluted him, even though he was in civilian clothes. "I'd like to salute those boys when they salute me."

"Mr. President," he responded, "you are the commander in chief. You can do whatever you want."

Thus, on arriving on the south grounds of the White House, when the Marine saluted him, he saluted back. The young man didn't blink or look away, but you could tell by the look on his face he couldn't believe it. Five minutes after the President left, he probably ran to phone his mother and tell her the president of the United States, his commander in chief, had just returned his salute. The word spread like wildfire through all the services— the President was saluting back.

It was a great practice and one that he considered vital to the morale of the armed forces. When newly elected President Bill Clinton called him to ask for his advice on being president, one of the first things Reagan told him was, "When the members of the armed forces salute you, salute back." Clinton started doing it right away.

It was a practice, however, that was going to cause me some anxious moments.

One cool autumn day, we were at Camp David when I nearly had a heart attack. Around five o'clock that morning, the U.S. Park Police and I took Gimcrack and the other horses we were going to ride that day out of their training barn and then transported them by truck to Camp David. Once there, we had them ready and waiting for the President, First Lady, and agents to ride. I had Bear, my wonderful, big, and powerful Park Police horse who would literally walk through fire for me if I asked him to.

The U.S. Park Police has been very fortunate in obtaining horses. Ninety-nine percent of these horses have been donated, which is perfect, since it cannot afford to buy and train horses. They are mature horses and have been either racehorses or fox-hunting horses. For one week, the Park Police will evaluate a horse to see if it can be used. If so, the horse is then issued to a rider and given rigorous training to perform their duties as U.S. Park Police horses.

After we had mounted our horses, we were off for our ride, leaving Camp David and going into the Catoctin Mountains of Maryland. The President was riding on my right side. As we approached the back entrance of Camp David, the Marine opened the long security gate. When we reached him, he made a very snappy salute and said in a loud voice, "Good morning, Mr. President."

The suddenness of the motion and the loud voice scared Gimcrack, and at once, the monster horse ducked and bolted off to his right. This massive animal was running at full speed on blacktop; if the horse had slipped, the President's brains would have been scattered all over the pavement. My heart was in my throat. Now Bear thought there was something terribly wrong, and he bolted too. The President masterfully gathered up his reins and brought Gimcrack to a stop, and I was able to bring Bear back under control also. If I had been on the President's other side, Gimcrack would have probably smashed right into me.

After we had recovered from our near catastrophe, my thoughts immediately turned to Mrs. Reagan. She looked right at me and said, "John."

"Mrs. Reagan, I'll take care of it." She had seen everything that had happened, and I knew exactly what she meant by that tone. She was thinking: *This is dangerous. What are you going to do about* this?

Concerned that this young Marine was going to salute like that again, I knew I needed to take care of this problem right after our ride. I didn't, however, say anything to him then. If you don't know horses, you won't realize that you're doing something wrong—how could you?

We continued calmly on our ride, and from then on, everything went according to plan. Behind Camp David, there is an old shack about which there is a story of a woman in the Civil War who would hide people there—probably slaves or others on the run. Her name was Lilly, and there is a legend that her ghost is still in there. Every time the President rode by he would call out, "Lilly, are you still in there?" Then he would begin the story saying, "I know I've told you this before."

"I'd like to hear it again," I would always say.

As he told the story, he'd look behind him so Mrs. Reagan could hear. "Yes, honey," she'd answer, "I know," and every once in a while she'd say, "Hi, Lilly."

When we returned from our ride that morning, I called the Camp commander of Camp David. I said, "We need to sit down and talk."

"Fine, John. Can you come to my office?"

"Yes, sir." I always showed these guys the utmost respect. Although the agents are in charge, the Marines will do whatever we need them to do to complete the mission. They deserve respect.

When I arrived at his office, he had his executive officer

(XO) and the captain of the security detail there. He said, "John, tell us what happened."

I first explained to them how the President almost lost control of his horse and then said, "We can't have these guys saluting like that. I know you don't know horses. We are so lucky that the President didn't come off on that blacktop and split his head. That's how bad it is. I cannot express it any deeper. It's very, very dangerous."

"John, you don't understand," the lieutenant said. "These guys live to salute their commander in chief."

"I understand perfectly. I was in the military, and I know what that means. So let's work this out." From then on, anyone standing post when the President was going to ride would be briefed in advance.

The next time we were at Camp David and approached that back gate, the President was gripping his reins a little harder, and he was getting a little deeper in his seat. We approached the Marine, and, as usual, he said, "Good morning, Mr. President," but this time in a low voice as he saluted *very* slowly. The horse looked at him as if he couldn't care less. The President saluted back, and after we got through the gate, he looked at me and winked.

I then turned to Mrs. Reagan and she gave me her smile of approval. Earlier that morning before our ride, Dennis Ayers rode my horse and I rode Gimcrack to the back gate where the Marine and I rehearsed how the "Good Morning" and salute would go.

The commanding officer was waiting anxiously for me when we finished our ride. "How did it go?" he asked.

"It went *great*." I jumped off my horse, and shaking the officer's hand, I said, "The President really wants to keep doing that. He loves saluting the men."

RONALD REAGAN loved thoroughbreds in part because of their incredible physical ability. I remember a story he told me about his days in Hollywood when he had roles as a young cowboy. During the filming of *Santa Fe Trail*, they went out to the hot Arizona desert to shoot some of the scenes. Errol Flynn was the star, playing Jeb Stuart, and Reagan was with the Confederacy, cast in the role of a young General Custer. The director told Reagan that if he brought his own horse out to the desert, he would receive an extra twenty-five dollars a day. Wanting not only to make some extra money but also to ride his own horse, he brought a big, black thoroughbred. All the movie extras, who were wranglers looking to pick up some extra money, were kind of pooh-poohing this "Hollywood glamour boy" with his elegant horse. They were all on rough and tumble quarter horses.

When they started to film the chase scenes, however, Reagan, on his thoroughbred, would just take off and would keep going. He literally left all those quarter horses and the camera truck in the dust. "Cut!" yelled the director. They would have to film the scene again and again and again. After the third time, the director said, "Ronnie, can't you slow that horse down?"

"Yes, I can," he answered, but by that time, the quarter horses were so tired they couldn't do it anymore. "After that," the President told me, "I got a lot of respect from those cowboy wranglers."

One of the things he loved to do most on a horse was jump. For those of us in the Secret Service, that was a nightmare. Here you had the leader of the Free World atop an eleven hundred pound animal, flying over logs and bushes. He'd jump over logs the height of coffee tables, and while we were frightened to death that something might happen, it was obvious that he just loved to do it.

Under certain conditions, any horse will jump. It just depends on *how* he jumps. If he gets into a situation where he has to jump, he most often will. Horses are born with that instinct. The President would stand up in his stirrups, put his knees into the knee roll, lean forward, get ready to jump, and take off. When the horse landed, he would ease back into the saddle. He did it with perfect rhythm. It was beautiful to watch.

After each jump, he would get a big smile on his face. There is something about jumping that can be so satisfying: the thrill of the unknown. The simple fact is that no matter how good the horse or how many times you have made a given jump, there is still *the* question: Is he going to make the jump or not? I may do everything the right way, and still the horse might not take it. That is the rush. You could put a heart monitor on the President or me, and every time we would jump, the needle would go right up into the red zone.

The key to success in jumping is never to let the horse see any of the apprehension you may feel. When you tense up, the horse senses it. If you start getting nervous or scared, that signal goes right down the reins into the horse's mouth and into his brain, and if you are on an English saddle, the horse can feel you

just as well as you can feel him. The natural tendency is to
squeeze harder when the horse starts running faster, but if you
do that, he's going to go even faster. You must *never* show your
fear. I think the manner in which the President handled his
horses translated into the way he worked in the realm of politics.
Like him or not, he was always calm and resolute even in the
midst of a crisis. I think his experience with horse riding was
something that he applied to his political leadership—always let
everyone know that you are in control.

However, as much as the President loved to jump, it still
presented an enormous security challenge to us. I made the decision to go to him with our concerns early on. I gingerly raised
the issue with him, and he kind of nodded and then moved on.
During the next trip to the ranch, as we were getting ready to
ride, he pulled me aside. "Say, John, you know that conversation
we had last time?" Even though he didn't say what that conversation was about, I knew exactly what he was talking about.
"You know, riding is dangerous enough. So for the good of the
American people, I just don't feel like I should put myself in further danger by jumping. What do you think?"

"Sir, every time you take that jump, I have to take it with
you. So on behalf of the Secret Service, I thank you, because I
don't want to be jumping out there either."

He laughed and then broke the news to Mrs. Reagan.
"Good," she said with a smile. Likewise, she had never liked the
fact that he jumped.

In 1987, I was transferred to the WPD where I was put in
charge of the security at Rancho del Cielo. I brought my thoroughbred with me from the East Coast. He was a racehorse that

I had raised, and later I rode him in the foxhunts. Ruler of the Roost was his professional name, but I just called him Ruler. His great-grandfather was Bold Ruler, who had won the Kentucky Derby years earlier.

I tried to change Ruler into a Western pleasure horse, but that proved to be a mistake. One of the big problems with him was that he had very tall withers, making it difficult for me to find a saddle that would fit him. A Western saddle would clamp down on his withers and that could cripple him. One day, when I was in the tack barn soon after I had moved Ruler out West, the President asked me about him and whether I had solved the Western saddle problem. I explained to him that I could not find a saddle that would fit him. "Let me show you something," he said, gesturing with his arm. I followed him over to one of his saddles. It was a J. W. Capriola saddle, distinctly different from other Western saddles in that the gullet was much higher. It had been made in Elko, Nevada, and on it were his name and the date (1980). The President said, "This will clear the withers of a horse like yours. Why don't you try it?"

I did, and it fit beautifully. The next time we were together, he asked, "Well, how did it go?"

"It went great," I told him. "That saddle fits Ruler like it was made for him. I'm going to have to buy one of these."

"For what?" he asked.

"Because it fits the horse, and I can't find anything else."

"Well, no you don't need a new one. You've got one now." That was his way of saying he was giving me the saddle.

"Are you sure, Mr. President?"

"Yes, it's yours."

The President had other pursuits that he enjoyed. He occasionally golfed and was pretty good at it. One of his friends was Walter Annenberg, a philanthropist and billionaire who made his fortune largely in media and real estate, and was appointed ambassador to Great Britain by Reagan. One day, we were out golfing on his private course at his estate *Edenbrook* in Palm Springs, California. This course had been designed by an expert and was considered one of the most challenging courses in the country. Annenberg was obsessed with it. He had an army of grounds keepers all dressed in brown slacks and short-sleeved shirts with pith helmets on their heads, walking around and making sure everything was in order. When a dead fish turned up in one of the ponds, the alert went out, and they scrambled to remove it as soon as possible.

Annenberg explained to the President that he wanted the course to be perfect. "I won't let Chi Chi Rodriguez play here anymore." Chi Chi was then one of the top golfers in the country.

"Why not?" asked the President.

"Well, he takes up too big a divot on my fairways."

Nothing else was said, and then Reagan got this devious grin and turned to me, "John, what time are the horses coming in?"

Annenberg's eyes suddenly got very big. I knew exactly what the President had in mind, so I joined in.

"Sir, you said after lunch."

"Okay," he said. "Where are you going to unload them?"

"Well," I said, glancing over at Annenberg, "you said to unload them on the second tee. This is where we'll unload them. You want to ride them down the fairway here?"

By this time, Annenberg was just dying. I am sure that he

had visions of the President turning his number two fairway into a polo field. Reagan carried the story on for a few more minutes before he finally let Annenberg off the hook.

While the President loved his horses, he wasn't overly emotional about them. I remember it was a few days after Christmas 1982, when I received word that his black beauty, Little Man, had fallen and broken his neck at the ranch. We were all at the Annenbergs' beautiful home in Palm Springs again. I knew that I'd have to break the news about Little Man to the President. With hesitation, I walked into his bedroom early in the morning where he was in a bathrobe lying on the bed reading a book. "Mr. President, we have a problem with Little Man. Your vet tells me that he has fallen and has a broken neck. He recommends you put him down."

After a few moments he asked, "Well, is the vet sure that it's broken?"

"Oh, yes. It's Doug Herthel." He is one of the best veterinarians in the country.

"Okay, then. He's the doctor. I don't want the horse to suffer." That was the end of it.

Reagan didn't say another thing about Little Man's death until we returned to the ranch. Soon after we got back, he went up to Boot Hill, a beautiful vista on the ranch where he buried all the animals. He found a flat stone and chiseled Little Man's name on it, his date of birth, and his date of death. He labored on that stone for quite some time. I was surprised by all the work he was putting into it, and I offered a modern solution. "You know, Mr. President, you could get one of those electric drills to do that."

"No," he said, chiseling away, "I want to do it by hand." It was clear to me that although he didn't express his emotions about the horse in anything he said, the time he spent working on that rock said, "This horse deserves my labor of love."

If you go up to Boot Hill, you will see all sorts of graves—for cats, dogs, and horses. Each one has a chiseled rock that marks their passing. In addition, each stone was hammered and placed there by Reagan.

In all the time that I spent with him, I only saw him emotional a few times, and when he was, it was only for a short period. It wasn't that he was cold; just the opposite. He was very warm, but he'd take the finality of death as "this is God's way." As written in Mary Beth Brown's book *Hand of Providence*, "God has a plan and it isn't for us to understand, only to know that He has his reasons, and because He is all merciful and all loving we can depend on it. That there is a purpose in whatever He does and it is for our own good."

UNLIKE MY early exposure to horses in Boston, Reagan didn't start riding as a young boy. When describing his earliest experiences on horses, Reagan later recalled, "First I felt a little uneasy, but then I realized: horses can be very loyal friends." It was during his time as a radio broadcaster at WHO radio in Des Moines, Iowa, that he first actively and frequently rode. Joining friends at the nearby Valley Riding Club, his love affair with horses began.

In the 1930s, he enlisted as a reserve cavalry officer at Fort Des Moines to take advantage of the opportunities to ride. He made it into the reserves by faking an eye test (he already had poor eyesight). Later in an interview with biographer Lou Cannon, he called joining the reserves "one of the smartest things I ever did."

By the time he was in the army, they were phasing out the horse cavalry in favor of tank units (Fort Riley, Kansas, still had a cavalry horse facility in the 1960s), but there were still some horse units in the army, and he was in one of them. Years later, after I had known him several years, he gave me his copy of the *Cavalry Officer's Horse Guide*, thinking I would find it interesting. The guide laid out everything the army thought you needed to know about horses and cavalry tactics. It was well thumbed through, and there were a few Reagan doodles inside of it. He knew all of the diagrams: what your position should be during a cavalry charge, how to jump, and how to prepare the horse. The training requirements were quite amazing. You had to ride around a rigorous course, jump over several obstacles, and maintain control of your animal at all times.

Unlike people who learn to ride as a hobby or as a sport, learning to ride in the cavalry makes you a very disciplined rider. They rode in McClellan saddles, which are very uncomfortable. (This saddle was designed to do those fifty-mile treks back in 1865 with General Custer!) Similar to an English saddle, the McClellan saddle has an even harder seat. It has clips on the back for the bed roll, and a scabbard for officers to put their swords in. Occasionally, cavalry officers were expected to ride in those saddles twelve to eighteen hours a day. You can tell by how the President carried himself in the saddle that he was that kind of a rider. His back was ramrod straight, and he was squared up on his horse, confidently in control of his animal. Only when he jumped would he lean forward, and that was to carry the horse over.

The President usually rode English, which meant he controlled the horse with direct rein. If you want to go to the right, you pull your right rein. To turn left, you pull the left rein. With a Western horse, you have neck reining, which means you lay the left rein across his neck to make him go right. Furthermore, when you ride English, you use your legs to apply different amounts of pressure to move the horse in the direction you want him to go. It's called balancing the horse. In Western riding, your feet dig deep into the stirrups, toes are up and heels are down at an eight-degree angle. In English riding, you look down and see the very tip of your boot, no more.

Riding English is physically demanding, and it's a style of riding for the benefit primarily of the horse. If you start trotting in the Western saddle and know how to ride, you're just sitting in the saddle. With an English saddle, you post. As the horse comes up, you come up with him. You put a little weight in your stirrups and rise above the saddle. When the horse comes down, you relax your legs and you come down. It's poetry in motion when you do it right.

On an English saddle, you run up the stirrups on the billets, the piece of leather that holds the stirrup. While the stirrups are metal, I always like to have the rubber inserts. The President had rubber inserts that said "Property of President Ronald Reagan." One time I put them into his stirrups, and I ran them up. He would, however, always run his billets through where the pad was, because he didn't want a pad. He's from the old school when you didn't have pads, but I like the pad because it makes your grip a little better. The President's stirrup had little pointed bumps, which is what kept his foot in there. That was how he wanted it, because that was how the cavalry rode.

If anybody has touched my saddle I can tell, and so could he. You know your stuff, and you know how you like it. So that day when he went to get his saddle, right away he asked, "What's this?"

My only thought was, *Oh, no!*

He said, "I don't use rubber."

"Sir," I responded, "I did that. I thought you'd like it for the grip."

"Oh no, no, you don't do that." So I took them out, and he said, "See? Because this is how I like to run my stirrups up, putting the billet through the opening in the stirrup."

"I know you do it that way. I just thought— Well, I wasn't thinking."

Reagan's saddle reflected the fact that he was a serious rider with little interest in show. The saddle he used was a Parianni forward seat jumping saddle, which was made in Italy. He bought it as a young man, and by the time he was president, it was more than thirty years old. A Parianni saddle is small and has minimal padding. While most people would find it quite uncomfortable, for him, less was more.

Whenever he would come to the ranch, he would dust it off and clean the billets by hand. The saddle was old, but it is such a good, well-made piece of leather that it will last forever. Occasionally, some stress-point stitching would come loose. I'd take it to Jedlicka's, and my friend Si Jenkins would have it fixed and back to me the same day. Other times, I would secretly use some saddle soap on it when I cleaned mine, just to keep it in great shape. One morning he said, "I think a little elf's been touching my saddle." That was his way of thanking me.

"Well," I said, "we have got to catch that little rascal one of these days, Mr. President."

It was a great saddle—simple lines, no frills or decorations. President Reagan had other saddles, as well. The Queen of England gave him a beautiful Steuben saddle made in Germany. A very functional saddle, it was a piece of art. The king of Morocco also gave him a saddle as a gift. It came in this beautiful rosewood box, and when you opened it up, the aroma of leather was simply tremendous. It was very fancy, with detailed stitching. The breastplate had Reagan's initials on it engraved in gold. We used that saddle once on a ride. After the ride, the President asked me what I thought of the saddle.

"It's a beautifully constructed ornate saddle," I said, "but that's where it ends."

"I agree. Let's just put it back in the box." He immediately returned to the saddle that he knew and loved.

Besides his saddle, the President cared about his pants: he wore English riding pants. The Filipino Navy stewards who were assigned to care for the President's wardrobe and personal needs didn't know exactly how to care for them. One day when he came out in those pants, I looked at them and raised an eyebrow. "I know, I know," he said to me.

The other agents had no idea what we were talking about. The stewards had ironed the pants and had put a sharp crease in them. You never ever put a crease in those type of pants.

"Well, I guess that I'm stuck with these pants," he said before mounting his horse and riding off. Knowing the President would not want to hurt the stewards' feelings, I knew he would not say anything about it. I got word back to the stewards not to iron his riding pants.

One of the most important things the President learned

while in cavalry school was that you take care of your horse at virtually any cost. For the horse officer, the horse was his life. If he couldn't stay with his horse for at least twelve hours a day, he was no longer a cavalry officer. He was a foot soldier.

A good horse can make an average rider a better rider, but a good rider with an average horse will bring out the best in that horse. When you get in from a hard ride, you are tired, thirsty, cold, and wet. Even so, you always attend to your horse first. You don't go near a glass of water, and you don't do anything until you've taken the saddle off, cooled your horse down, rubbed him down, and given him some water. Only after he's been taken care of and turned out should you take off your boots, get some food and water, and get out of your wet clothes. That was the way the President always took care of his horses.

People often assume that at the ranch we saddled the horses for the President and First Lady. The fact is, the Secret Service is not responsible for things like that. We are there to protect him, and we will only do something (as with the wood chipper) if it is a threat to the president. So Reagan saddled his own horse, and he wouldn't have wanted it any other way. There were, however, a few exceptions when he was delayed because of presidential duties, which would have held the ride back if we had waited for him to saddle both horses. In those rare instances, I tacked them up. When he came out and saw both horses saddled, he looked at me and said, "Oh, good, thank you. Now we're back on schedule."

After a ride, the agents would wash the Secret Service horses. This did two things. It cleaned the horses, and it allowed the agents to run their hands over the horses to detect if there were any problems with them, for example ticks. I wanted them to get to know their horses. The agents would then tie them, scrape the excess water off them, and let them stand until they were dry before they turned them loose. If they let the horses loose before they were dry, they would roll in the dirt and have sand sticking all over them. Horses love to roll.

One time there were four agents who had already tied their horses up, and they were scraping the excess water off them, when one of the agents put his hat on the fence post. I said, "Charlie, don't put your hat there."

"Okay," he said, putting it back on his head. At that point, I went into the command post. Looking out the window, I could still see the guys working on the horses, and Charlie had placed his hat back on the post. Suddenly, a gust of wind came up and blew the hat off the fence post into the horse's face. The horse went nuts. He reared up and pushed Charlie away from him. With his incredible strength, he ripped a two-by-four off the fence post. Now you had a scared horse with a two-by-four hanging from his lead rope with nails sticking out of it. Panicking, the horse started running around the paddock area. I ran from the command post and leapt over the fence and into the corral. Running toward them, I told everyone to stand still. Miraculously, the horse stopped. Gently walking toward the horse trying to calm him down, I cut the lead rope, freeing him from the two-by-four.

I just looked at the other agents and said, "This is a perfect example of what I've been trying to tell you guys—how strong these horses can be and how dangerous they are. I'm sure you'll agree that it is really fortunate no one was hurt. This could have been a disastrous situation." After that episode, I noticed they were more cautious working around the horses. The word about the incident was passed to the other riders.

President Reagan took care of his horses. Before every ride, depending on what needed to be done to clean the horse, he would grab his currycomb and a brush to lift the dirt off the horse. Then he would go to a softer brush to clean the more sensitive areas of the horse. It's a ritual between the horse and rider. Reagan took his work very seriously.

Still, this can all be dangerous work. You need to clean their feet and press on the hooves to make sure that the shoes are on correctly. How the horses are shod is very important. You can cripple a horse if the farrier does not shoe him properly. Since humans take horses and ride them where horses would not normally go, they need iron shoes on their feet. Wild horses do just fine without them because their feet grow very hard, and they know where to step, but domesticated horses go where their rider tells them to, and so they need their shoes replaced on an average of every six weeks.

When I pick up my horse's feet, I start with his right front foot. When I'm done with the front feet, I walk to the rear, and by the time I get there, my horse is already picking up his back foot. It's difficult to pick a horse's back feet up if he doesn't want them picked up. While I always start with my horse's right foot, President Reagan would start with the left foot and then work his way around. Any horse has the propensity to kick in a given situation. When working around a horse, you should always stay close, touching him to let him know where you are. If he does kick, you will be pushed away instead of being hit with the full force of a kick.

Oftentimes people will leave their horses in a stall. If you let them out in the pasture, they can get into more trouble. President Reagan always wanted his horses running free. They might get a few nicks on them and tangle up their mane and tail, but they are better horses if given some freedom. That was the way he wanted it.

5

The Cowboy's Lady

Most special friendships have a memorable beginning. For some, it was the right word spoken at the right time. For others, it was an unexpected event that brought two people together who might otherwise never really have gotten to know each other. My bond with Mrs. Reagan was sealed a few months after I began riding with her and the President. One cool spring morning, the three of us went riding on the back trails of their ranch. We were heading out on the inside of what was known at the ranch as Pennsylvania Avenue. This path was separated by barbed wire, the same kind you would find on any ranch. As we continued off onto another trail from the Avenue, the road was getting narrower and the brush was getting thicker. I had not gone this way before. This was early on, before we had all the markers in place. As we turned at a crest in the trail, we came to a spot with barbed wire on our left side and thick heavy brush on our right. There was now only a small narrow path on which to ride.

The President was out in the lead, and it was at about this point when he asked, "What do you think, John?"

"Well, if we go too much farther and it keeps doing this, we're going to have to turn around."

"Well, that's all right."

"Yes, sir, it is."

We continued riding and soon there was brush sticking out. As we approached an even narrower passage, still moving alongside the barbed wire fence, I said, "We can't go through there like that because of the barbed wire. We're going to have to literally push through the brush a little bit." The brush was just little twigs connected to larger branches hanging down, so you could actually duck and go under it. I thought that the person who was most vulnerable was the President since his horse was the tallest.

Rick Williams, a tall Texan, was the agent on the team that morning who was riding closest to me. I said, "Rick, I don't know what's on the other side of that. Will you go through there and kind of break up those branches a little bit so we can see what's on the other side?"

After making his way through, Rick called me on the radio. "It's okay. The brush is not that bad, and on this side it's clear. You are going to have to put your hand up to push the brush aside, but it's easy going."

"Okay, Rick," I said. "We're coming through."

I then told the President, "Sir, it's okay for us to go through. It's a little brush we need to go through, but on the other side it's clear."

The President rode out first, following the path. He pushed the brush aside, but it then came right back. I am still not sure what exactly happened after that. It might have been that the brush came back while at the same time the First Lady's horse, No Strings, who was behind the President's horse, veered off to the right taking her through some very thick brush. No Strings, a powerful and big but gentle quarter horse, just kept walking, and as he was walking, the brush and branches began scraping her. While the horse moved farther, Mrs. Reagan was being forced off the saddle by the brush. The brush was literally pushing her off the back of the horse. "Whoa! Whoa!" she cried out.

Riding behind her and seeing all this happen, I tried to determine in a split second what would be the best thing for me to do. I couldn't get my horse there in time, and I couldn't stop her horse. Soon I was going to be in the thickets too, making everything worse. My adrenaline kicked in and took over, and I literally dove off my horse. You know the stories of the mother who lifts a car to save her child? Well, that was what was happening to me. I was younger at that time and was in good shape. By now Mrs. Reagan had been peeled back so far that she was falling off her horse. Diving toward her, I literally caught her in my arms. Boy was I lucky. It was something right from a Hollywood stunt scene.

Grabbing my neck, she hung on to me tightly. For me, she was light as a feather. I slowly lowered her down, as we were still clinging together. I was holding her, the First Lady, and I was trying to comfort her. While she was not crying, she was really close. Startled and frightened, she was shaking—like anyone would be. All of this happened so fast, but it seemed like an hour. Finally I said, "You're okay, hon. I've got you. Let me see your face. There are no scratches on you, nothing, no blemishes." Immediately after I said it, I caught myself—I had just called the First Lady of the United States "hon." It bothered me because I felt that I had crossed the line. I had not meant it out of disrespect. I was simply trying to comfort her, but you were not supposed to say that sort of thing.

Wanting to reassure again, I told her, "You're okay. There's nothing wrong. Do you want me to have you driven back to the house, or do you want to go on?"

"I want to go on," she answered.

"Good for you. You come off the horse, you get back on."

She was really shaken. Although some of her clothes were torn a little bit, she was all right. I put her back on No Strings, and she bravely continued on the ride without saying another word about it.

The President hadn't seen or heard what had just happened, and Rick had no idea what was going on. They were just wondering why we were taking so long. Only the agents behind us that day saw the event unfold, but they weren't able to get to us in time to help.

Nothing more was said until we got back from the ride. It was during lunch that Mrs. Reagan told her husband what had happened to her, and after they had finished, a call came through on the red phone. When the President picked up the phone on his end, the red phone in the command post would immediately ring. The agent who answered the phone told me, "The President wants to see you in the tack room."

I went down to the barn, figuring he had a horse question, but just before I entered, it occurred to me that it might be about what had happened on the ride that morning.

The President had changed into his wood-chopping gear—jeans, boots, cowboy hat, tee shirt, and gloves. "Say, John," he said in a kind and gentle manner, "Nancy told me what you did out there, and I didn't see or hear anything, but she could have been seriously, seriously hurt, and you saved her."

"Mr. President," I said, "I was at the right place at the right time."

"How *did* you get off that horse so fast?" the President asked.

"I jumped off. I didn't throw my leg over. I just literally dove off, and I landed right under her and caught her."

"Well, John, you saved her from possible injury, and I am very grateful."

"Sir, any of the agents that were with us today would have done the same thing if they were in that position."

"Yes, maybe another agent would have done it, John," he said as he pointed his finger at my chest, "but *you* did it."

Many years later, Mrs. Reagan and I did talk about that incident. I reminded her that I had called her hon, and she just said, "That was all right."

THE FIRST TIME I was actually around Mrs. Reagan was when I was covering the president-elect at their Pacific Palisades house after the election. I recall my first impressions of her—at all times, she was poised and elegant. The fact that I would soon be covering her as part of my detail was another one of those turns in my life that I never expected. Our first trip together was to one of her favorite stores in Brentwood, her old stomping grounds. Sometimes she liked to go to that store by herself, and there everyone knew her. People would say things like "Hi, Mrs. Reagan," and "God Bless you, Mrs. Reagan." Besides a few greetings that she enjoyed hearing, no one really bothered her. She had been going to that same store since her days as an actress.

I was in the down room and the closest agent the morning she wanted to go, so the detail supervisor told me that I needed to take her and that he had a car and a driver waiting for her use. Since the trip was unannounced, it was considered a spontaneous or off-the-record movement. An agent didn't need to go there in advance, and no one at the store needed to be notified. I introduced myself to her and said, "I am the agent who is going to take you to the store."

"That's nice," she said, and that was about it.

The next time she and I were brought together was on inauguration day. Many people have seen a picture of the outgoing and incoming presidents standing side by side near the double glass doors at the White House, awaiting their armored limo for the ride to the U.S. Capitol where the new president is sworn in. Behind President Carter and President-elect Reagan were the two First Ladies, awaiting their limo. That was the post they gave me. The cars were in front of the main entrance of the White House on Pennsylvania Avenue, and I was just leaning against the car the First Ladies would be riding in. The Secret Service agent driver was in the car.

It was a typically cold January day in Washington, D.C., but the mood was electric. Finally, the two men emerged from the White House, and they were escorted to their armored limo. Following them were their wives, who stood waiting at the top of the stairs. Mrs. Reagan looked right at me and said, "John."

Shocked that she remembered my name, my first thought was, *Is she calling me?* When I realized that she was speaking to me, I looked directly back at her and said, "Yes, ma'am?"

"Is that the car that we're supposed to go in?"

"Yes, ma'am, it is, and I'll be going with you."

"Okay. Should we come now?"

"Yes, ma'am." I also clearly recall Mrs. Carter turning to her and saying, "You know the names of your agents?" I worked with Mrs. Carter a little bit, and she too was a very gracious lady, but everyone was different, and each had his or her own style.

Little was said to me during the short drive up Pennsylvania Avenue. The two ladies were talking in the back. I had my earpieces in, and at first there was a lot of traffic and then it died down. Before any event, the advance agent always schedules a briefing period for all the agents who will be on duty. The information at the briefing is related to the type of crowd there is going to be. For example, a speech on a campaign stop will warrant quite different preparations than an appearance at the Kennedy Center. Nonetheless, agents are continually on the lookout. There are intelligence agents in the crowds and agents on the perimeter peering through binoculars. The Inauguration is a very special event. For months, agents have been prepared. Every inch near the president has been gone over. Hundreds of agents are on duty, and there are vehicles and even helicopters standing by.

After President Reagan was sworn in, he and the new First Lady started the traditional parade back down Pennsylvania Avenue. Both sides of the street were lined with crowds of enthusiastic people cheering and waving. I worked the left rear of the President's armored limo. It was a long but very exciting day.

That night, all the grand inaugural balls were in full swing. After attending just the first few, I could sense we were entering a new era. Washington, D.C., hadn't seen this much excitement or style in years. Soon, America would feel good about itself again, and that was because of President Reagan.

We made our way to each ball—something like twelve or fifteen of them. Getting the new president around to them was like navigating a logistical maze. While the agents are responsible for getting the president safely to his destinations, his staff actually determines when and where he is going. The agents are always working with the staff to make sure things run smoothly. I worked the whole day and night. The next day, George Opfer, the agent in charge of Mrs. Reagan's detail, said, "You worked the night shift to the inaugurals." This, I later found out, was a prestigious shift.

I covered the First Couple at every ball, and everywhere we went there were celebrities. They were all dancing—Frank Sinatra, Jimmy Stewart, Dean Martin, and people like that whom I've always admired. The main entertainment was at the Capital Centre, where there was standing room only. I was sitting with Frank Sinatra, Dean Martin, the Osmond kids, the President, and Mrs. Reagan. Perry Como was good friends with Mrs. Reagan, and he looked great.

I had been a fan of many of these stars, and now I was getting to watch them operate up close. They were all very gracious. I remember there were times when someone would get up and I'd move around, trying to keep my position, and I'd feel like I was in the way. I bumped into Frank Sinatra a couple of times, and he was so apologetic, thinking *he* was getting in *my* way while I was doing my job. I said, "Mr. Sinatra, you're not in my way. It's crowded and I bumped into you because it's crowded, not because you're in my way. You just do what you need to do, and I'll work around you and everything will be just fine."

The Reagans loved these performers, and during the week of

the inaugural festivities, some of their friends were invited to the White House. One afternoon, Perry Como and Frank Sinatra were rehearsing some songs and duets. Mrs. Reagan said, "I want to go down and hear Perry and Frank sing."

I asked, "Perry and Frank who?" I didn't even know they were in the White House at the time, since they were scheduled to perform in the evening.

Now sensing a great opportunity, I said, "Well, I think I will join you for that one." When we entered the room where we usually have black-tie dinners, I saw them singing and playing and kidding back and forth. To pay tribute to the new First Lady at the festivities, Sinatra had changed the lyrics in the song "Nancy with the Laughing Face," which he had written years earlier for his daughter Nancy's birth. I thought that was a great song.

There were three nights of attending one ball after another. To me it seemed as if it went on and on. Then things settled down and the day-to-day responsibilities began. The Western Protective Division (WPD) worked to protect the President's children and the ranch on the West Coast, while the Presidential Protective Detail (PPD) covered the White House. Garrick Newman was the assistant agent in charge on this detail, and in 1984 he would become the agent in charge of the WPD.

A ranch trip was scheduled soon after the inaugural ceremony. This would be the Reagans' first trip to the ranch as President and First Lady of the United States. Mrs. Reagan asked me if I would be going to the ranch with them. "Yes, Mrs. Reagan," I told her, "I will be there."

She just smiled and said, "Good." In retrospect, our relationship started right away. During the first days of the new presidency, I actually spent more time with her than I did with the President while we were on the East Coast.

THE FIRST FEW TIMES I went riding with them, the President and First Lady rode side by side, and I rode behind the President. His horse, El Alamein, was so difficult that if he had broken while I was behind him, I probably would not have been able to catch him either until he had stopped or until the President was hurt. Sure enough, we soon had a small incident that required my assistance. El Alamein had managed to get the bit under his tongue. When that happens, you do not have full control of your horse. I knew something was wrong, so I rode up from behind the President and said, "Mr. President, I think that bit's under his tongue."

"Oh my goodness, I'll get off."

"No, sir," I said, "don't you get off your horse. Don't get off. I'll get it." I opened El Alamein's mouth, and I slipped the bit up.

"Oh, thank you, thank you very much," said the President.

The First Lady just kept looking at the President and then turned toward me, considering what had just happened.

Not long after that, we were on another ride, and the President had a question for me. I rode up right beside him, and at that moment, the First Lady dropped back. I looked at her and then moved back to my position behind the President. "You stay up there with my husband," she said. "That's where you belong. I want you beside my husband. I can't help him up there the way you can."

"Oh, Mrs. Reagan," I said, "you know, you're like two kids—holding hands, riding down the road. I think that's wonderful. I don't want to interfere with that. I'll do my job riding behind him."

"Yes, John, I appreciate that you want us together, but, no, you are going to ride beside him." I think she appreciated my conversations with her husband, and she was making it perfectly clear that that was what she wanted.

"Yes, ma'am."

I told my boss that, and he said, "Good. That keeps you even closer to him." The President understood this point as well.

Sometimes, we would ride twenty yards ahead of even Mrs. Reagan, and literally, no one could hear what we were talking about. He'd tell stories, and at times he'd say something that would strike me as funny. Although he'd be laughing, I'd still be looking around, doing my job. Mrs. Reagan would ride up from behind and ask, "What are you boys laughing at?" She called us the boys. The President loved that, and I liked it too.

Mrs. Reagan appreciated particular personality traits. She would ask me certain questions, and I would say, "I don't know," while other people would say they did know when they didn't. That was a big mistake, especially with her. Some people would try to ingratiate themselves with her, and that got them into a lot of trouble. She is a smart lady, and many times she would ask a question that she probably already knew the answer to.

Several times, the big boss would send me down to talk to her about something. "Why are you sending me down?" I'd ask.

"Because you're the only one who can talk to her," he'd answer.

"That's not true, sir. That's not true at all. Just tell her the truth." Also, there were times when I'd tell her, "Mrs. Reagan, you can't do that."

"Why?" she'd ask. I would explain why that situation wouldn't work, and she'd say, "Okay. Thank you, John," and that would be the end of it.

Sometimes, she would ask the agents to do something that was not necessarily in our job description. She did this at the ranch because there was no staff with her on the property. She would go to the Secret Service knowing she could trust us to give her the right answer or to get things done. To their credit, she trusted the military aides also.

While Mrs. Reagan did not love the ranch as much as the President did, she loved being there because it was solitude, as it was for the President, and she was with the man she loved. She liked the privacy and time alone. Still, she would be on the phone a lot. She had her schedule and her homework. Her staff would tell her that she needed to look at papers, and the charity requests were endless. It takes time to consider each one thoughtfully. The First Lady can stay as busy as she wants. Everybody always wants her for something, no matter what party she's in.

She also truly considered the ranch as something they had produced together. "Ronnie made this with his own hands," she would say.

There are two bells at the ranch. One is outside the residence and the other is near the tack room. Mrs. Reagan's grandfather had been an engineer, and the bell by the tack room is the one that he had on his locomotive. Federal Express shipped it out to the ranch in this big wooden crate. It was huge and weighed a ton. When the bell arrived, we all thought, *What are we going to do with this?* but the President built a stand for it and placed the bell on it.

When he had Mrs. Reagan's horse, No Strings, ready for a ride, he would ring that bell and that was her signal to stop what she was doing, leave the house, and walk up to the tack room. After the ride, she would go back down to the house, and he would stay up top with the horses or in the tack room. Soon after, she would ring the smaller bell by the house, and that was his signal to come down for lunch. He would stop what he was doing and usually say, "She wants me. It's time for lunch."

So here was the president of the United States, who could talk to anyone in the world via satellite through the WHCA, using bells. Those two bells were reserved for just him and Mrs. Reagan, and they were never used for other things.

Often, the President and Mrs. Reagan were like two kids sneaking around, stealing kisses. He would call up to the command post and say, "We're going for a walk."

The supervisor would say to us, "We've got agents in position so give them their room and let them have their privacy."

With his cowboy hat tilted and his boots on, he would hold her hand and walk around the ranch. They would relax, sit or stand in the grass, and just talk. Sometimes they would go paddling around on the pond in their canoe, on which the President had painted the words "Tru Love." Because canoes are a little tricky and can easily tip over, they did not do that very often. It was, however, something else they enjoyed together. So that Mrs. Reagan could get in, the President would walk out into the water up to his waist and steady the canoe by the dock he had built by hand. He was enormously proud of that dock.

Before a ride, everything was readied in a very systematic way. The agents rode horses purchased from Stu Gildred, a local rancher. Before the President arrived at the ranch, Stu would have the four horses delivered for the agents, and after the President left, he would have them taken back down to his ranch where he would care for them. Once in a while, if I had a good rider with me, I would call Stu and say, "Meet me at the Aisal Ranch at the Refugio Road." I would then, along with another agent, pony the horses up, which means leading a horse. It took about two hours to get the horses up the path to the ranch, and it was difficult to do. I did not mind, though. Since I was riding, it was fine with me.

Not wanting to use the President's land, we did that for years until one day he said, "Why don't you leave the horses here." That did make things a lot easier.

Then there was the issue of the hay. The President had more horses than the agents did, and he didn't think it was right for his horses to be eating more of the hay. I suggested, "Why don't we just put it all together, and we'll pay for the hay we use." The President still wanted to keep things separate, because he didn't want the taxpayers to pay for his horses' hay.

The horses were always running free, and before the President came to the stables, the caretaker would put hay in the stalls so the horses would know it was feeding time. What stall each horse would go into had been all worked out. El Alamein had picked his, and no other horse challenged him for it. The horses trotted in from the pasture in order of their rank and then walked into their stalls to eat. Once they were all in, the caretaker would shut the gates so they'd be ready for the President when he arrived at nine o'clock in the morning.

He'd always get Mrs. Reagan's horse, No Strings, first. No Strings was given to her by their friend Judge Bill Clark. A long-time family friend since the 1960s and fellow Ranchero, both Bill and his father had been judges appointed to the California Supreme Court by then Governor Reagan. Bill served as chief of staff for Reagan in Sacramento, later as the President's national security advisor in Washington, D.C., and during the President's second term he was the Secretary of the Interior. For some time, the President had been looking around for just the right horse for Mrs. Reagan. When Bill found that out, he contacted his friend at once and said, "I've got one for her. This horse has taught my kids how to ride. He's big and strong, but if you drop the reins he will just walk down the trail."

"Okay," the President said. "How much do I owe you?"

"Mr. President, you don't owe me anything. I want to give him to you."

"Well, I don't want any strings attached to this." That was where the name No Strings came from. That horse was a godsend and a great horse for her. He was big and she was peanut-sized. Still, she could handle him, and they got along very well.

There was a ritual the President followed every time he rode. Once No Strings was ready to go, he would next tack up his own horse, El Alamein. After tying each horse to their respective hitching rails, he would walk over to the huge bell and ring it. This was an announcement to her that the horses were ready. He was like clockwork. If he said it was time to ride at 9:26 a.m., that is when we would start the ride. President Reagan hated to keep anybody waiting.

Mrs. Reagan and the President enjoyed their morning ride together. Always dressed for the ride, she'd have her little babushka on and a hat for the sun. One time the President had a little melanoma removed from the tip of his nose. The doctor told him, "Make sure you always have a hat on." He normally did anyhow.

In the early days, he'd wear his cowboy hat but then later gravitated to the Secret Service baseball caps. We'd be riding and he'd be looking at me. He would say, "You know what I'm doing?"

"Yes, sir."

"What am I doing?"

"Sir, you're looking at my face because we're in the same position, and you want to see where the shadow's hitting so your nose is covered."

"That's right." I'd sit back and ride, not even realizing at times how close we were. It just came naturally, the two of us, an amazing situation.

The First Couple again had a routine when the ride was over, and to make certain everything went safely, I planned my own routine. I would always be in a position in which I would get off my horse as quickly as I could as we rode in. I would then go and stand by the President so I would be near him when he dismounted his horse. He would take his right leg and throw it over the horse's neck and jump down from a sixteen-hands-high horse. I could never do that, even on my best days. Besides, I wouldn't want to do it. Out of the hundreds of times he jumped, only twice did he waver a little bit where I had to put my hands up to steady him. He would just look at me and say, "Thank you."

Next, he would put the halter on his horse and tie him to the hitching post. Mrs. Reagan would just wait patiently atop No

Strings. That was her assignment. Finally, he would walk over and help her off her horse. She would swing her right foot across the horse's neck like he did, while he held her by the waist. One day, her spur got caught in the reins. I just took the reins and released them, and she continued with her dismount. The President knew what I had done, and he looked at me appreciatively.

He would still be holding her by the waist as she slid down the horse and into his arms. They would stand there kissing like two teenagers at a drive-in movie. It was actually a little embarrassing. I would turn away giving them more privacy. Embracing her, he would stare at her after they kissed. It was the same after every ride.

One morning, a new agent who had been assigned to Mrs. Reagan during the ride caused a minor disruption in the routine. When we got back from the ride, the President jumped off his horse and tied him to the hitching post while the agent assigned to Mrs. Reagan was off his horse and standing next to her.

Holding up his hands to her he said, "Ma'am, I'll help you down."

I watched as the President looked over with genuine hurt on his face. "John, that's my job," he said.

The agent didn't hear any of this and reached over to grab Mrs. Reagan by the waist. She resisted, knowing that was her husband's job.

The President rushed past the agent and said, "This is my job." She slid down into his arms and they kissed. He then looked at the agent and asked, "I suppose you were going to do that too?" The agent just stood there red faced. I later explained to the President that it was my fault that I had not briefed the agent on how Mrs. Reagan dismounted, but the President just laughed.

After the President would unsaddle No Strings, Mrs. Reagan would get a towel and wipe down her horse. One thing she always had to do was feed No Strings a carrot. She would hold the carrot in her hand while she was rubbing him down. I said, "You know, Mrs. Reagan, you might not want to do that. See what he's doing? He knows you've got that carrot in your hand so he's fidgeting and he's putting his head as far back as he can to try to bite the carrot while you're wiping him. He might grab it pretty quickly, and I don't want the possibility of him biting you accidentally."

I'd stick the carrots for my horse in my back pocket because I didn't want to feed him until the bit was out of his mouth, he was unsaddled, and I'd cleaned him. Sometimes I'd clean his hooves after we rode, and it was then he'd see the carrots and would reach right down and take one out of my back pocket. I'd just laugh because *I'd* made a mistake.

The President would give a carrot to each of the agents to feed to their horses after the morning ride. I once informed him that the agents were waiting to feed their carrots to their horses until after they had walked them up to the corral and had taken their bridles off. I then teasingly told him, "Mr. President, Agent Bill Corbett does not feed the carrot to his horse. He eats the carrot himself." Bill's face turned red.

Handing Bill another carrot, the President said, "Here's another carrot for you so you can give the other one to your horse." He always had a solution.

Mrs. Reagan appreciated the horses because they made the President happy. Her friends did not ride. In fact, like the President's friends, they were all amazed that she would like it, but she did. While riding, she would just look around and be in her own little world. She and the President didn't talk much while on their horses. She left the riding schedule and routes all up to him. That was his domain.

The ranch and the riding were his passions, and she loved to see his enthusiasm. When they were riding, he would point out the things he saw to her such as where the flowers were or the shapes of trees or the areas he had cleared earlier.

"Yes, dear." She would wink at me, and then he would wink at me too.

She learned to ride because she wanted to be with him. She once told me the story of how she connived her way into spending more time with him years earlier. Back when he was dating her, he spent a lot of time on the back of a horse. So she would ask him to take her riding, even though she didn't ride well.

I could see that these were two people who were very different, but very much in love. There was no one they would rather spend time with than each other. Mrs. Reagan adored him. He could lift her spirits even during the bleakest of times with a few words. When Mrs. Reagan had to have her mastectomy because of cancer, it was very traumatic for her. The President saw her grief and tried to console her. "Well you know, dear," he told her, "I've always been a leg man." That made her laugh.

If there could possibly be any complaint about their relationship, maybe it would be that she was overly protective of him, but is it considered a fault to be too good to someone? They were completely devoted to each other, and at times I felt like I was coming between them during the rides. She often told me, however, that my being there made the President happier, and that made her ecstatic.

The President always considered Mrs. Reagan before a ride. He knew she didn't want to run, she didn't want to jump over a fallen tree, and she didn't want to be out there for four hours. Those times, we would go alone.

We would also ride alone if the weather was a little nasty. He would go out in inclement weather that she wouldn't want to ride in. Before he left, though, she'd make him put on his jacket, gloves, hat, and scarf. Then she'd come out and say, "John, I'm just not going to ride today. I don't want to, it's too wet out, but he's going to ride."

"I wish I could stay back with you," I'd say. "I think it's too wet out too."

She laughed. "You're not staying back."

"No, ma'am, I'm not."

6

Protecting the Rider

There is a big difference between being someone's protector and being his friend. I considered the President a friend, particularly after he left office, but I never let it interfere with my assignment. Since emotions can cloud decisions and friendships are bound to create emotions, it is best to keep them completely separated. This was hard for some of my friends to understand. After Reagan left office, I commissioned Keith Christie, a famous cowboy artist and friend, to paint a portrait of the President and me riding, which he completed in June 1998. I sent him a number of photos of us riding so he could get started. Days later, he called wondering how to draw me. "John, I've looked at all these great pictures of you with the President, and it's obvious he's talking to you or he's pointing something out or he's laughing. He's either talking, pointing, or laughing, and you're never looking at him. You're never smiling."

"Keith, I'm doing my job," I reminded him.

During the time we spent together the President would tell me a story or ponder aloud something that he saw. While I listened to everything he said, no one would *ever* find a picture of me looking at him while we were riding together. I was looking for possible danger. I was his protector first, his friend second.

This wasn't always easy. In the Secret Service, we've strict orders to do our protective work and our protective work only. Sometimes, though, the lines can be somewhat fuzzy. What classifies as protective work?

One of the first times I was alone with the President in the White House was on the Saturday or Sunday after he had been sworn in. I was at F-1, which is the Secret Service post right next to the President's private elevator. It was seven o'clock in the morning, and I heard the elevator doors open. There he was in his suit, his arms full of Paul Rossi statues. The Annenbergs had put twelve beautiful bronze statues on permanent loan to the President—one with a rattlesnake, another with a bucking bronco. Those statues were heavy, and he was almost dropping them.

"Good morning," he said. (He always said it first to everyone. He was just that way.)

"Good morning, Mr. President. Where are you going?"

"I'm going over to the Oval Office to put these in there."

I could tell that he was struggling with them. "Sir, can I help you?"

"Well, I know you're not supposed to have anything in your hands in case you have to draw your weapon to protect me."

"Sir, we're in the White House, and it's very secure. I think it would be okay for me to carry a couple of those statues for you."

"Well, okay, I'd appreciate it."

I notified the command post that we were moving and then carried a few of the statues for him into the Oval Office. Was this technically my job? Some people might say no. In this case,

I determined that the President had a need and might have hurt himself. Therefore, I considered it part of my job.

PROTECTING ANY president is a difficult and complex task. The commander in chief is constantly moving, giving speeches and shaking hands. That is a given in any protective work you are doing for the president. You are forever trying to protect him from "The Jackal," a universal name taken from the movie that is given to any potential assassin, and in order to be ready to meet this threat, members of the Secret Service are always planning and conducting advance work.

How the president chooses to spend his off time presents additional challenges. During the Ford administration the Secret Service contacted the Boston field office to supplement its PPD. Still living in Boston and working as a member of the Counterfeit Squad, I was temporarily assigned to the protective detail at that time, and my task was to protect President Ford's son Michael and his wife, Gayle, who lived in the Boston area. Michael was attending Gordon-Conwell Theological Seminary, and while he was in school, I would sit outside his classroom. The Fords were avid skiers, and when they got together, it was always in Vail, Colorado, during Christmas where they hit the slopes. I would be in the command post that had been set up in one of the chalets, while the agents who were skiing with them would contact us so we could plot exactly where the First Family was at every minute while skiing.

In 1978, I was transferred to Washington, D.C., where I officially became a permanent member of the PPD. There I was assigned to protect Carter. While covering him, fishing was the leisure activity that received most of our attention. Carter loved to fish, and he liked to take trips from the presidential compound at Camp David to go fishing in trout streams. Once when he was in the stream, he was complaining that all the Secret Service agents standing around might be scaring the fish away. So we stepped back a little bit to give him more privacy, until the current pulled him under. He was wearing wading boots, and we worried that they might fill up with water. Fortunately, he resurfaced and everything was fine.

By far the biggest challenge we encountered was protecting President Reagan while he was on his horse. You can carefully check out the ski equipment and do an analysis of the snow conditions to make sure that the chance of an avalanche is remote, and you can check out a lake or stream to determine how quickly the water is running and where the sharp rocks might be, but you can't tell how a horse is going to behave on a given day. He is a large, powerful, breathing, *thinking* animal. Riding horses is by far the most dangerous recreational activity any president has enjoyed. Soon after President Reagan came into office, the hard and complicated question was posed: How are we going to handle this?

The Secret Service doesn't have any horses, and at that time, it didn't even have a formal training program for agents to learn how to ride. My boss asked me to look into this, and the U.S. Park Police is where I went. Why the Park Police? For one thing, they had beautiful horses, and they would ride their enormous, impeccably trained thoroughbreds through Washington, D.C. They were used during large demonstrations (there is always some kind of demonstration going on in Washington) to keep the crowds under control. Normally, horses are trained to move away from pressure. However, because of their crowd-control duties, Park Police horses must instead learn to move into pressure, not away from it. There are seven stables located in the Washington area, and these horses must become accustomed to the city environment. Part of that environment is the hard surfaces of the city, so barium is placed on their shoes, which prevents the horses from slipping.

I contacted the Secret Service Liaison Division, and they set up an appointment for me to meet with the chief in charge of the Park Police mounted units. Chief Parker Hill and Jack Fish, regional director of the U.S. Park Police, met with me at their office. "The Secret Service is in a predicament," I told them. "This President rides. He rides a lot, and he rides heavy. We don't have the horses, the time, or the facilities needed to maintain the horses. Is there any provision under which we could train on and ride your horses?" The U.S. Park Police are by law obligated to support the U.S. Secret Service. Technically, the White House grounds belong to the U.S. Park Police Service.

My next conversation was with Dennis Ayers, the sergeant in charge of the training barn. An ex–Marine corporal, Sergeant Ayers looked the part of a rider. He had thick silver hair and was six feet two inches tall. It was obvious he was in shape. We called him the "Silver Fox," "silver" because of his hair, "fox" because of his agility on horses. I told Dennis, "We need to devise a method where agents can train on your horses to protect the President of the United States, and we need a horse for him."

He looked at me suspiciously. "Do you ride?"

"Yep."

"Well, then, let's go for a ride."

Dennis took me down to the stalls to show me around. The Park Police have a gorgeous old training barn, with block wood in the stalls and sliding wooden doors with bars. At the time, there were forty horses in the barn and an indoor ring for training when the weather required it.

Next, he strolled down to the end of the barn and called out an order to one of the officers, "Bring out *Bull*!"

Moments later, out strutted this enormous seventeen-hands-high dark bay stallion, snorting and pounding on the walls like a stud horse often does. My eyes got really big. "Man," I thought to myself, "this guy's gonna kill me."

"Sarge, I've never used full reins like those before."

Dennis looked at me. "All of our horses ride like this. If you can ride, you can ride one of these. Now we're going for a ride in the woods." I knew that he was testing me, and I also knew that I couldn't back down.

Nervously, I climbed on top of Bull, and Dennis and I headed out into the park. We rode around for a couple of hours through Rock Creek Park, through the foot and bike paths, the open areas, and the wooded areas. Then he said, "Let's pick up the speed." So we got into a canter, and Dennis headed straight for a fallen log. He jumped, and I was right behind him. Never having jumped that high before while on a horse, I didn't know what to do. Fortunately, I safely followed him over the log. After a couple of hours of this, we returned to the barn. "I now know that you can ride," he said. "Now we're going to take the next step."

Together, we devised a plan to train agents for riding with the President. The U.S. Park Police had an extensive 480-hour training program that they put all of their mounted officers through. "We don't have that kind of time," I told Dennis. "We have to do it in a three-week period." Everything had to be accelerated.

From the very beginning, it was a challenge to determine who might actually be a possible candidate. If you ask the typical agent whether they can ride, most of them will say yes. They will say that whether they have ridden regularly or whether they just sat on a plow horse when they were twelve years old and that was it. Will Slade, who was the supervisor at this time, figured we could solve the problem by asking them a simple question: "How many minutes have you been in a saddle?" I would ask them. "Ten minutes? Ten hours?" We finally whittled down the possible candidates to those who had spent a fair amount of time around horses. Then we gathered them at the training barn for the three-week course.

One of those in that first class was Big Jim. Jim Davidson had played football for the Los Angeles Rams and was huge. If he had wanted to, he could have picked up one of those horses. We brought those fire-breathing thoroughbreds out and guided them into the ring. I asked the agents who wanted to go first. Big Jim said, "I do," and walked confidently up to one of the horses. He pulled himself on top of the animal and somehow got the horse to walk around the ring. I knew at once, however, that this was going to be trouble. Big Jim did not really know what he was doing.

"Okay," I said, "go into a trot." He had no idea what that meant, but he pressed the horse hard and it began to canter instead of trot. Big Jim was getting scared now, so he squeezed even harder. The horse started to take off and was soon running around the training ring. Having let go of the reins, he was now holding on to this massive horse by its neck. The other agents were all standing outside the ring watching this horrific scene and thinking, *Oh my God*.

Big Jim was squeezing the horse harder and harder trying to get him to stop, but the horse wasn't going to stop. He was just going to run faster and faster. Jim started to slide off the horse, and before we knew it, not only was he holding the horse's neck, but he was wrapping his legs around it too.

Ralph Pfister, one of the Park Police training officers, and I were standing in the middle of the ring. I turned to him and asked, "Ralph, how are we going to handle this? How are we going to stop his horse? He's going to get killed out there." We decided we had to slowly step in front of the horse. Everybody thinks that if you get in front of a horse he will turn. That is not necessarily true. By this time, Big Jim was *underneath* the horse's neck, and his feet were around his withers. He was literally dangling upside down.

Ralph and I approached the horse cautiously. As we got closer to him, we were talking softly, trying to get his attention. The monster finally slowed down and then stopped. He was probably getting tired from carrying Big Jim around his neck. Big Jim dropped to the ground, and the thoroughbred just stood there staring at him. I then turned to the other agents, "Okay, who's next?"

"Not me," they all said at once.

Eventually, we did get all the agents out and on the horses. Training for them was difficult, regardless of what kind of physical shape they were in. Riding a horse requires that you use a lot of muscles you otherwise don't use, and most of the agents were in serious pain after riding horses day after day. We would go out into Rock Creek Park, and Dennis would lead the way. When he turned his hat around, everybody moaned, "Oh no," because that was the clue that we were going to start running.

For the next half hour, we would have to keep control of our fire-breathing animals while we ran them, racing through brush and ducking tree limbs.

Next, we would take them through and over a series of obstacles. During one of our runs through Rock Creek, an agent, Carl Stickane, was crossing a bridge when his horse drifted. Suddenly we all heard a splash. Looking in the creek, we saw Carl under the water with his huge horse on top of him. He couldn't breathe, and his horse was on his leg. The Park Police helicopter *Eagle One* was called in, while everyone was wondering what to do. It was Dennis who suddenly reached down, grabbed the horse's rein, and pulled the massive animal up. Though cold and shaken, Carl was not seriously hurt, fortunately.

"Carl, do you want to continue this?" I asked.

"Well, maybe I'll take a couple of days off."

"Sorry, we can't do that. We don't have time. Either you continue or you don't. Not continuing is okay."

"I want to do it," he said.

"Okay, then be back here at six o'clock tomorrow morning."

The next day, Carl showed up on time, ready for another day on his horse. When he opened his locker to get his riding gear, inside he found a scuba diving mask, flippers, and an oxygen tank with a note that read: You may need this if you decide to go diving with your horse again.

Our agents were determined to make it through the program, but it was tough. One of them hit a tree and had to have a major knee operation. Still, during these tough three weeks, all but one agent survived the training. He was continually coming off his horse and finally came to me and asked, "Should I stay in the program?"

"You will have to make that decision yourself," I told him. "I'm not going to tell you you can't do it. The fact is, you've come off your horse several times during training—on the obstacle courses, in the open woods."

The next day he came back and said, "I don't think I can do this."

The peer pressure to stay in the program was enormous. In a matter of only weeks, we had a great group of agents assembled for the sole purpose of protecting the President while on horseback.

Dennis selected the first U.S. Park Police horse for the President to ride at Camp David and possibly other locations. He asked me to come to the training barn to show the horse to me. "What do you think, John?" He was a seventeen-hands-high Hanoverian named Giminish.

"Well, Dennis, the President will need to try him out." I asked my boss to go to the President's staff and request that they make time for him to come to the training barn. There, Dennis and I introduced him to Giminish. President Reagan tried him out and liked him. I wasn't surprised—I knew the President's liking for big flashy thoroughbreds. He rode Giminish for the next two years.

When Giminish came up lame, Dennis again came through for me with Gimcrack, a seventeen-hands-high thoroughbred who had been given to the Park Police by Abdnor Smith from Hickory Tree Farm in Middleburg, Virginia. The President rode Gimcrack for the rest of his days in the White House.

MAKING SURE that we had trained agents to ride was one thing, but then there was the problem of the ranch itself. We brought all the training officers to the President's ranch to show them the type of terrain we were faced with, so they could better understand our challenges.

The fact that the President had a 688-acre ranch didn't make things any easier. Early on, we developed an elaborate system so we could track his movements. We needed to know exactly where he was in case assistance was needed or he came off his horse. The problem was solved when Agent Win Erickson devised a brilliant plan after he had spent three months at the ranch working on his idea. He had presented two plans before this one to the President, and both had been rejected. However, the President approved his third plan.

Instead of putting up ugly street signs on such beautiful property, Win took some of the rocks from along the trail and drilled numbers into them. Those markers blended in so well that unless you were looking for them, you couldn't find them. To be able to follow the markers, a map had to be constructed, and members of the Department of the Interior came to the ranch to draw one. When I announced that we were moving from marker forty-two to marker forty-three, the agents at the command post knew exactly where we were when they looked at the map. If I said, "Rawhide is down, we need evac!" they would know which marker and which Emergency Landing Zone (ELZ) we were closest to. (Years later I would use those exact words, but at a different ranch.) The ELZs were permanent, cleared-out areas where *Marine One* could land safely. The President thought the plan was ingenious.

We did all we could to make certain the President and First Lady could still have some privacy at the ranch. Still, there were preparations for everything. When the President wanted to go for a ride, we would look at the big map in the tack room as we figured out which route we were going to take. The map had been divided into four sections. Once it had been determined where we were going to ride, escape routes had to be identified as well as ELZs for evacuation. I was always trying to plan ahead—if something happens here, how will we fix it? I had it all figured out as best I could.

When the President had a trip to the ranch on his schedule, I would travel out there four days in advance to work on his horse and scout the property. I would labor eight to ten hours a day, making sure that El Alamein was all ready to go. If there was a problem with the horse tack, for example, if the stitches were coming lose from the cinch, I would take it to my good friend Si Jenkins and get it fixed. You should always check your stitching, especially at stress points. You don't want your equipment breaking loose while you are riding.

My preparations also included riding El Alamein. Initially, he would be feisty because he hadn't been ridden for a while. When you've a spirited horse, a rider will usually go through a routine. First, he'll tie the stirrups up and then use what they call a lunge line to get the horse to run in a circle. The idea is to get the freshness out of him. At the start, the horse will balk and kick when he does it. However, once the horse drops his head and starts licking his lips, he's calmed down a little bit and the rider can then get on.

The problem with El Alamein was, the more you worked him, the more excited he got. He was a beautiful horse on the outside, but inside he was just difficult. So I devised a game with El Alamein. I'd get on him and wouldn't touch him. I'd drop the reins, and he would take off, just running and running. If it got too dangerous I might pull up on the reins, but mostly I would just let him run, without touching him with my hands or legs. Suddenly he'd stop and look back at me as if wondering, *What's going on here?* If he could've talked, he would've asked, "What are you going to do?" He wanted a fight or a struggle from me, but I wouldn't give him one.

Then he would run again, uphill and along the trails. On reaching the top of the hill, he would stop and look at me again. He would be breathing hard now because he had been running quite a distance. This would go on for two hours or so, back and forth across the ranch. Finally, after all of that running, he would slow down to a canter. This was a ritual that would play out for four days.

Environmental conditions at the ranch could be tough on the horses. Because it was so arid, special care was given to their hooves so that they wouldn't be damaged by the dryness. I would put a mixture of tar and hoof dressing on El Alamein's hooves. This mixture soaked into the hoof wall. I also saw to it that the water troughs were purposely overfilled. That way, when the horses came to drink, their feet would be in the mud and would soak up some of the moisture.

By the time the President arrived, El Alamein would be in great shape: calmed down, vigorously run, and *somewhat* under control. If the White House photographer was also making the trip West, I would wash El Alamein and tar his feet. I would wet his mane and tail, pour some Quicksilver on them, and then rub it in. Quicksilver is a brand name of a product that works like hair conditioner. You rub it on the horse, leave it on for about five minutes, and then rinse it off. Although my fingers would turn blue, both El Alamein's mane and tail would be a beautiful silver, as soft and fine.

Was this officially part of my job? No, but if my president was going to have his picture taken with his horse, I wanted that horse to look darn good.

Along with getting El Alamein in shape, I'd also have the agents and special officers patrol the perimeter of the ranch before the First Couple flew in. We were looking mostly for footprints. Had there been anybody up at the ranch? Occasionally someone on a mountain bike would climb one of the fences and go for a ride. I don't think they even knew that they were on the President's ranch. Secured by the WPD, there were twenty-six special officers with one agent in charge covering the property even when the President wasn't there.

El Alamein was a beautiful horse, but because he was big and gray—almost white—he would stick out. I realized I needed to talk to the supervisor of the countersniper team, who had positions set up around the perimeter of the ranch. There were three teams, and each one was responsible for a particular sector. Their job was vitally important: they were constantly looking through their scopes and binoculars for potential snipers in the surrounding hill country. When they would see something, they would report, "I got motion in one or two." Immediately, the shooter would go to that spot with his scope and verify if there was something. Ninety-nine percent of the time it was an animal. Yet they were always alert, just in case it was a potential threat.

For each position, two countersniper team members would be paired off, a shooter and a spotter. The shooter looked through his scope and fired the weapon. The spotter peered through his high-powered binoculars and then told the shooter how to adjust his aim to hit the target. These teams were constantly scanning for possible snipers on another hill who might be gunning for the President. We would ride by them, and they would always be doing the same thing. The shooter would be lying on the ground; his rifle would be pointed off at the distance, resting on a rolled-up towel that was on a rock or log. The spotter would be standing, staring through his binoculars. They would never move from their location, and they would never remove their eyes from their scopes while on duty.

These guys are incredible. They can shoot someone at one thousand yards—the distance of ten football fields. Their weapons are made specially for them—the stock is shaped to conform to their cheekbones. The Secret Service has an expert gunsmith, and he is the only one—other than the shooter—who is allowed to touch these weapons. One time, a couple of guys from the countersniper team took me out and persuaded me to fire a few rounds. After the spotter looked through his binoculars, he laughed. "I can't even tell you how to adjust from that one." That response brought to mind my motto, courtesy of Clint Eastwood from his movie *Dirty Harry*, "A man has got to know his limitations." I knew mine. I was not trained to shoot at a thousand yards. I was trained to shoot no farther than fifty yards.

So I went to the countersniper team supervisor and asked him about El Alamein. Was it a problem that the President was riding a gray-white and that I was riding a brown horse? "Everyone knows the President rides a white horse," he told me. "When the two of you are out there riding, we can't see your faces at a thousand yards. We can see your torso. We can see your legs, how you dress. While we really can't say which one's which, we do know he rides a white horse."

The President had another beautiful gray named Gwalianko, which I had been on a few times. I went to the President and said, "With your permission, I'd like to work him and see if he can be a protection horse for me."

Not asking why, he just shrugged his shoulders and said, "Sure."

Gwalianko was a great horse, and, soon after, we were both riding grays. From a thousand yards, you couldn't tell those horses or riders apart. I also made sure that my dress was the same as the President's. If he wore a ball cap, I wore one. If he had on short sleeves, so did I. Several photos of us riding these two horses side by side were taken for me. When I showed them to the countersniper guys, no one could tell the difference. By doing this, we had just reduced the chances of the President being shot by a sniper by 50 percent. Contrary to what you might think, a sniper would probably be unable to get both of us. Snipers only shoot one round in the chamber at a time.

It was a simple solution that I think worked quite well, but it was not the sort of solution that you mentioned to your mother. While I was living in Washington, D.C., my mother came for a visit. She was an excellent cook, and after my shift, some of the boys came over, and she made dinner for all of us. I had a picture displayed that the White House photographer had given to me of the President and me on our white horses, riding side by side, wearing similar clothing.

"Isn't it cute?" my mom said to one of my fellow agents. "My son rides the same color horse as the President."

"Well, do you know why he does that, Mrs. Barletta? At a

thousand yards, a sniper can't tell the difference. There's a fifty-fifty chance that they'll shoot John instead of the President."

My mom was a little shocked, and as I walked by, I said to the agent, "What a lovely story to tell my mother."

Whenever the President did go out on a ride, a veritable army of agents would be ready and available if they were needed. The President and I would ride out front, followed by Mrs. Reagan and the agent assigned to her. Behind them rode two more agents and a military aide. (The military aide was carrying the briefcase called the "football," which contained the codes to launch America's nuclear weapons.) The Secret Service would drive behind all of us in a Hummer. Initially, they used a Jeep to follow us, but it couldn't keep up because of the difficult terrain. In an effort to solve that problem, the Hummer replaced the Jeep, but it couldn't keep up either. It would get dented and stuck in the mud. Finally, Chrysler sent out its head mechanic and showed us how to use a Hummer. That seemed to do the trick. The President's physician, Dr. John Hutton, usually rode with the agents. Next in line behind the Hummer was the WHCA vehicle. Inside this vehicle was the communications personnel.

The Secret Service Command Center kept track of everything we did. It was located on a hill, away from the house. Hidden from view by some of the grand oaks on the property, the building was just a simple metal structure. Inside, however, there was everything from weapons to advanced communications equipment that wired the President to the world. These electronic devices were the state of the art in the 1980s. There was also an exercise room, a down room for the agents, and toilet facilities. In all, three metal buildings called Quonset huts, which the Navy Seabees had constructed, were on that hill. Besides the command center, there was the building that housed the doctor's supplies and special medicines as well as the offices of the military aides. The third structure served as the staff office and was where the President delivered his Saturday radio broadcasts.

During Reagan's tenure as president, there were communicated threats that we had to worry about. There was one man nicknamed "The Jackal" who was a viable threat. Trained in the military, intelligence determined that he had access to state-of-the-art weaponry. He wanted to kill the President, and our intelligence division worked hard to track him down. Finally, they caught him in New York. The American public heard very little about it.

Another incident of serious concern came quite by accident in the President's first term during a visit by the Reagans to the Augusta National Golf Course, where the prestigious Masters is played, on the invitation of Secretary of State George Schultz. While they were on the golf course an intoxicated man broke through the club's gates, driving a pickup truck. Somehow he ended up walking into the pro shop with a gun and took four people hostage. Among those caught were Lanny Wiles, staff assistant to the President, and Dave Fisher, personal assistant to the President. Lanny had a WHCA radio and was able to inform them of the situation. We evacuated the President and Secretary Schultz to the armored limo. Mrs. Reagan and Mrs. Schultz were out shopping when we heard the news, and they were taken to my hotel room.

Lanny started talking to the intruder to gain his confidence, and he convinced him to let Dave and the two women hostages go. The intruder then told Lanny that he wanted to speak with the President. Lanny contacted WHCA, and the request was for-

To John Barletta ~
Thanks for the Escort
Down Pennsylvania Avenue, 1/20/81

Ronald Reagan
Nancy Reagan

The inaugural parade down Pennsylvania Avenue in January 1981. I am at the lower right, wearing a red tie.

Getting El Alamein ready to ride at Rancho del Cielo ("Ranch in the Sky").

The main entrance of the rustic Rancho del Cielo. Reagan built the fences himself.

Riding at Camp David in 1981.

Riding Giminish in front of the stables at Camp David.

U.S. Park Police training barn in Rock Creek Park, near D.C., where the Secret Service trained to ride with the President in 1981. I am third from the right.

The first graduating class of the United States Mounted Secret Service, 1981. I am standing at the left, wearing the white cap.

Riding with Secretary Bill Clark and Senator Laxalt at Quantico, 1981.

Reagan, myself, and fellow agent Will Slade with Gwalianko in 1981.

A member of the Royal Canadian Mounted Police presents President Reagan with a horse as a gift from the Canadian government.

Sharing a light moment with Mrs. Reagan in front of the tack barn in 1982.

After I came off my horse and broke six ribs in 1982, Nancy Reagan gave me a gag gift of a seat belt.

Riding with Prince Philip in his carriage at Windsor Castle, 1982.

Christmas at the White House, 1982.

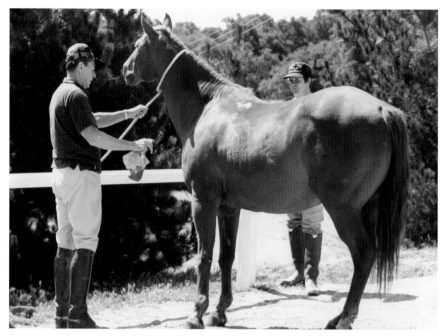

Treating Dormito with fly spray before a ride in 1983.

Joking around near the gas pump at Rancho del Cielo.

Marine One arrives at the south grounds of the White House in 1983. I am behind Mrs. Reagan.

At Andrews Air Force Base, Reagan pays respects to the flag-draped coffins from the bombing of the Marine Corps barracks in Beruit. I am walking behind the Reagans, next to the Marine.

Riding with the President at Rancho del Cielo in 1984.

My horse was selected to look like Reagan's horse El Alamein to confuse potential assailants, 1984.

Riding Gimcrack at Camp David, 1986.

The United States Mounted Secret Service in front of the south side of the White House during a training day in 1986. I am third from the right.

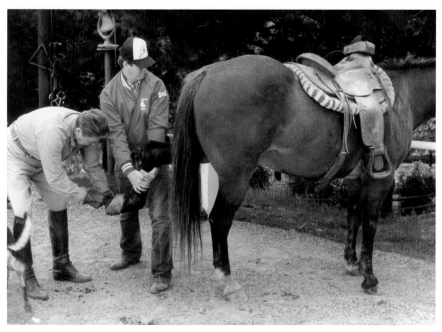

Holding No Strings's hoof as Reagan cleans it, 1986.

The President and Mrs. Reagan in front of the stables at Camp David in 1986.

Reagan and I in the Oval Office, 1987. Some of the Paul Rossi statues can be seen on the shelves and the table behind us.

Discussing the route of the day's ride at Rancho del Cielo, 1988.

Saying hello to admirers after landing at the helicopter pad at Rancho del Cielo, 1988.

Riding The Fonz while the President rides El Alamein at Rancho del Cielo, 1988.

Reagan visiting Ahead with Horses, a charity that allows physically and mentally disabled children to ride, in 1992. He donated two horses to them.

Reagan's visit to Russia after his presidency. I am at the right, in the second row.

Enjoying a fishing trip in Alaska in 1992.

warded to the President, who was still in the armored limo. Although the Secret Service discouraged it, Reagan agreed to talk, thinking of Lanny's safety. He got on the radio and said, "This is Ronald Reagan," but the intruder hearing the voice became too nervous to respond—twice.

Finally Lanny said to the man, "We need another drink. How about I go out and get us another bottle of Jack Daniels?" The man agreed. When Lanny exited the pro shop, the SWAT team grabbed him and brought him to safety. Next they entered the pro shop, disarmed the man, and took him into custody.

Then there was the ever-present threat of potential attack by our Cold War enemy, the Soviet Union. Whenever the President visited the ranch, Navy intelligence would report that the Soviets had placed a couple of their submarines just off the California coast in the Pacific Ocean. They were probably trying to collect intelligence. However, the Navy also believed that those submarines were carrying missiles and, in the event of war, would have orders to fire at the ranch. In an attempt to counter the threat of a military attack, the U.S. government reinforced portions of the ranch house so it could withstand a heavy blast. The reinforcements were made out of steel and concrete, and the reinforced area was called the "safe room." Besides keeping the President physically safe, it was important that all his calls to and from the ranch were also "safe." Audio countermeasures (ACM) allowed him to talk on his phone without his conversations being heard or intercepted.

The President certainly understood the need for security, and he never questioned anything that we asked him to do. There were times, though, when his sense of decency and kindness forced us to make some changes. One morning, we were out riding near the point called Lookout Mountain. This point offers a sweeping panoramic view of the ocean and the surrounding hills. If you look one way, you will see the Pacific Ocean and the Channel Islands. When you turn the other way, you will see the valley and all the trails. It was because of this vast, open space that one of the sniper teams always held its position at that location during daylight hours, continuously scanning the horizon.

As the President and I rode past the team on Lookout Mountain—we were maybe five feet from them—they didn't glance our way, even for a second. Although the President didn't say anything, I could just tell he was a little bit upset as we headed down the steep hill. "Is there a problem, Mr. President?" I asked.

"Well, they weren't very friendly."

I tried to explain. "Mr. President, they're doing their job. Their job is to look out that scope and make sure you are okay."

"Well, they could have taken a second to say hello."

After the ride I went to see the lieutenant in charge of the countersniper detail. "Who had lookout today?" I asked him. The lieutenant sent for the two men, and I tried to explain the situation to them.

"I've got a problem, but I don't know how to solve it. Please understand, you guys are very professional. I expect nothing else from you, but let me tell you what the President said."

After I related the story, the lieutenant shrugged his shoulders. "John, we'd love to sit and B.S. with the President. That would be wonderful, but—" I could see that the two sniper team members were worried.

About two months went by before we rode on Lookout Mountain again. We rode up the hill, and there, at the top, was the same sniper team that had been there the last time we rode by. I thought, *Oh, no, this won't be good*, but as we slowly moved by, the shooter and the spotter both glanced over and shouted, "Good morning, Mr. President," and then quickly went back to their assignment.

The President smiled at me and said, "That's better."

During a trip to Camp David in the early 1980s the First Couple went riding one cool, clear morning. The President was again on Giminish, the enormous dark bay thoroughbred that he loved to ride. I always tensed up a little bit more after we left the gates of Camp David. After all, inside the gates you had some pretty tight security. Once outside the property, however, you could run into anything—bow hunters or hikers. Whenever we planned to go riding near Camp David, the area we would be moving through was swept by the Marines an hour before we rode.

It was on that morning while we were riding through the heavily wooded area outside the gates that I suddenly saw something moving in the brush up ahead. It was a figure of a man, rising up and then ducking down again. I was riding next to the President, and I asked him to stop. "Mr. President, would you hold up a second?" He took one look at me and didn't say a word. Al Falcon, another agent, was behind me, along with a new young member of the team. Al was a great guy, a helicopter pilot in Vietnam, who was a first-rate agent.

I radioed him immediately. "Falcon, come up here right away."

"What's up?"

"There's someone out there, and I've seen him. He's not moving. You start walking your horse toward him, and I'll direct you where he is. Take your weapon out." He at once started moving slowly forward. We don't like to ride with one hand on these enormous horses, but he had his weapon out while I was talking to him on the radio.

"Go to your left a little bit. Straight ahead." Then I told everyone else, "I've got an unidentified target out there." The other agent slowly went up to Mrs. Reagan and moved in front of her. I got in front of the President to shield him. The rest of the agents formed a perimeter around us.

"He's about five yards from you," I told Falcon.

At that point he stopped and looked down at the ground. "Let me see your face, trooper," Falcon ordered. Lying there on the ground was a camouflaged Marine who had been assigned as additional security. For their training, the Marines are always told to *never* move while the President is in their area. Unfortunately, this young trooper made a mistake. I spoke to his commanding officer and tried to cut the kid a break, but the officer insisted that the young man be transferred.

In addition to the dangers of riding, the President's vigorous physical labor at the ranch was a persistent source of concern. For many political leaders, a round of golf at the club is a great way to spend some time outdoors, but Reagan liked to clear brush—and that presented its own unique set of problems.

Greasewood was what the President called it—low-lying brush that had an oily substance in it. If it wasn't cut back or removed, this brush could choke off trails, and it was a fire hazard. Sometimes the President would use a chain saw on it. Other times he would take a chain, wrap it around the trunk, and then attach the chain to a winch that was attached to the Jeep. He would press a lever on the winch, and it would slowly pull the roots out of the ground. I never liked watching him do this kind of work (imagine all that could happen!), but the President was insistent. One time, he attached the chain and then started operating the winch. Suddenly, the chain broke, and it came flying back toward us. No one was hurt, but I finally put my foot down. "That's it. No more chains. No more pulling the stuff out." He didn't say a word, and we never did it again.

Another problem was the wildlife. As I said earlier, there is plenty of wildlife at the Reagan ranch, and some of it can be threatening. The animal that worried us the most was the rattlesnake. There were literally hundreds of them on the ranch. They generally kept to themselves and never ventured near the Reagan home, but there were times when we were out riding that we would run across one.

Very few times did the President take Mrs. Reagan out for a drive in his beloved Jeep. It was an old banged-up vehicle, but he loved it. He would drive it around the ranch, using it to haul things like his pole saw, cutting saws, and buzz saws. However, one time after his presidency, he ventured out for a rare drive with Mrs. Reagan.

Usually I would sit in the front next to him, but since Mrs. Reagan was with us this time, I was seated in the back. We were driving down to Snake Lake, which is the farthest part of the ranch. Suddenly, we saw a rattlesnake lying in the center of the dirt road. Being cold-blooded, they often sun themselves in the morning. President Reagan stopped the Jeep because he did not want to run over it. He had this view about nature that we were essentially intruding on the animal's turf, and we needed to respect them. Whenever we ran across a gopher snake on the ranch—and there were plenty of them, at times measuring more than six feet long—the President would pick it up and move it to a more secluded place in the brush.

Before I had a chance to call one of the agents in the car behind us to ask someone to bring up a walking stick to push it out of the way, Mrs. Reagan firmly said, "John, shoot it."

"Mrs. Reagan, I don't want to do that." I explained that one of the agents could safely move it off the road with a large walking stick.

"John," she said, not budging, "it's a rattlesnake. *Shoot it*."

"Mrs. Reagan, there are hundreds of those out here. This isn't the only one. We're in the backcountry now."

Still trying to convince her that it made no sense to shoot it, she just kept giving me a look that said, "kill the snake." So I turned to the President, but he wasn't going to say anything.

I then tried to make an excuse. "Mrs. Reagan, it goes against my grain to take my weapon out in front of my protectees."

She continued to stare at me and again said, "Shoot the snake."

Realizing she wasn't going to change her mind, I radioed the vehicle behind us and told them what I was going to do. Then I pulled out my pistol and, from ten yards, blew the snake's head off. Nothing was said as we drove off.

A week later, I needed to inform the President of something while he was having lunch at the Los Angeles Country Club. Coincidentally, he had just finished telling his friends that story when I reached him. "That's the agent I was telling you about," he said. "That's the guy who shot the snake and blew its head off with a single shot. That's the guy."

The whole thing embarrassed me. Like all my fellow agents, I was an expert marksman, but the story behind the story is that in my .357 at the ranch I always carried one snake-shot round. It's essentially a baby shotgun shell, filled with pellets that spread out. You don't have to be that good a shot to use them. Did I ever tell the President? No, I figured that was one secret I could keep to myself.

PRESIDENTS ARE entitled to Secret Service protection for life, and one of the most difficult assignments that I faced came after the President left the White House.

His great friend, Bill Wilson, had access to a large ranch in Mexico through the Diego Redo family of Mexico City, and he invited the Reagans down for a visit. The two men had known each other since 1958. Wilson had introduced Rancho del Cielo to the President, and he had served as Reagan's first ambassador to the Vatican. I knew Bill as well, because he was a fellow member of Rancheros, and we both belonged to the Gringo camp. I enjoyed his warmth and good spirit, and when I wasn't on duty, I would see him socially from time to time. Once I was back on assignment, though, I tried to keep things strictly businesslike.

Planning a trip to Mexico was particularly difficult, because it was a foreign country riddled with problems. I sent an advance agent down to Fort Huachuca, Arizona, a U.S. Army base, to make preparations for our weeklong visit. Bill's ranch was in the middle of nowhere, and we needed to identify a location where a helicopter could land in case the President needed to be evacuated.

There was also the problem of the drug smugglers, and the fear was that if a drug cartel saw an American military helicopter flying overhead, they would think they were being raided and they would try to shoot it down. Our liaison division contacted the area police in Mexico and explained our concerns to them. They advised them that an American army helicopter would probably cross their borders at the location given, in order to assist the former U.S. president. They assured us that the helicopter would be cleared.

The ranch was enormous—eighty thousand acres of desert. I was a little anxious right from the beginning. Only Assistant Special Agent in Charge (ASAIC) Frank Domenico and I were going to stay in the bunkhouse, which did not have a radio or a television—nothing. The rest of the detail would have to make the one and one-half-hour drive on dirt roads to the ranch from Bisbee, Arizona, each day, crossing the border at Naco, Arizona.

After I took just one look at the horses, I knew that we were in trouble. The President was accustomed to riding thoroughbreds. These were rank horses. I examined their hooves and found they were shoeless and chipped up. As I looked them over more closely, my concerns grew when I noticed their ears and facial areas had nicks on them.

I immediately called Bill and asked, "Which one of these horses do you expect the President to ride?" While I was still looking the horses over, he came to show me the horse that had been selected for his friend. I said, "Okay," but I didn't want to tell him that the President shouldn't be on *any* of these horses. The President wouldn't want to hear that either. These two men were lifelong friends. They had been riding together before, and they were going to do it again. I went to Mrs. Reagan instead.

"Mrs. Reagan, these horses are terrible. I don't think the President should ride one. I damn sure don't want you riding one."

Mrs. Reagan just looked at me. "John, this is Bill." In other words, this is one of Ronnie's dearest friends. She did ease my concerns a little bit when she told me that she was not going to ride.

I just knew, though, that trouble was brewing. I feel very guilty now about what happened.

When you ride thoroughbreds, the rein is taut all the time. You're in spurs, and you're touching the horse with your legs to manipulate him. If you did that to these Mexican horses, they would go crazy.

These horses had been running free in this eighty thousand acre ranch. When Bill wanted to go riding, one of the gauchos would go out into the desert and just lasso him one. You normally don't do that to a horse. That's where the cuts on their noses and the nicks on their ears came from.

The riding was tough the first morning we went out. We were going up and down dunes, and as the President was moving down the trail, his horse started fishtailing. Unable to figure out what was wrong with his horse, he looked over at me. "Sir," I said, "just drop the reins," but he wouldn't drop the reins. Thoroughbreds react differently when you drop the reins; you can lose control of them. With quarter horses and Arabs like these, it's the opposite. You let them go and they calm down. The President had a very bad ride all that day.

The next morning, Frank and I had all of the horses saddled up. When Reagan came down, I told him, "Mr. President, I want you to ride this horse today," pointing to the one I had been on. "I'm gonna ride the horse you rode yesterday."

To let you know what kind of man this was, he told me, "John, but then you'll have a bad ride." He was willing to go back onto that same horse, knowing he was going to have a bad ride because he wanted me to enjoy myself.

I insisted, "Sir, you just take the one I rode. I'm gonna take yours. It'll be just fine."

So we switched horses and headed out again into the back-country. We were going down a hill ever so slightly when one of the bulls, which had gotten loose, ran by us about twenty yards off to the right. Moments later, the gauchos roared by us at a full run, twirling their lassoes in pursuit of the bull. The horses, thinking they were going to be roped again, started acting up and wanted to run away from the gauchos. The President checked up and pulled on the reins to prevent his horse from running, but his horse was insistent and started shaking his head and then bucking. This was not your typical crow hop, a gentle buck when a horse simply flips his rear end up. This horse had his head between his two front legs and his rear feet going straight up in the air. He was bucking for all he was worth, and the President was trying to hold him. I reached over and grabbed the back of his belt to try to pull him onto my horse, but my horse was going nuts too, and I lost my grip.

After the third buck, the President went flying into the air. He landed on one of the few clumps of desert that didn't have any cactus or rocks.

I jumped off my horse, as did Frank. I called on the radio for backup. "Rawhide is down." The follow-up vehicle, which was carrying agents came flying over the hill and literally went airborne. When they stopped, all of the agents bailed out of the vehicle.

The President was lying there in the hot sun and not breathing. Frank and I were getting ready to do CPR when he coughed. He was still not conscious, but at least he was breathing again.

We put the air mask on him, and his tongue was curled and his eyes were back in his head. I was thinking, *My God, he's got a spinal injury.*

Mrs. Reagan was advised of the incident and driven to our location. She was amazing. Although she was incredibly concerned, she knew not to interfere or ask any questions while we were doing our job.

The advance agent called for the helicopter from Fort Huachuca. I placed a cervical collar around the President's neck to stabilize him. Frank started going over his legs to see if he could find an injury.

All at once he came around. "I want to get up," he said.

"Mr. President, I don't want you to do that. I don't want you to move."

"What happened?"

"Your horse started bucking."

"Is it something I did?"

"No, no, you did it right. It wasn't something you did."

I was amazed that he didn't have a concussion, a broken back, or a broken collarbone. He had hit the ground with a heavy thud.

It took the helicopter awhile to arrive. He kept saying that he wanted to get up. By this time we had him on a backboard, and we moved him to an air-conditioned vehicle to get him out of the hot sun. Finally, the helicopter landed, but at a distance. It couldn't land on the terrain near where we were. We drove the vehicle the President was in to the helicopter, and four men carried him on the board while I held his head as we slowly walked him over to the helo.

There were just two paramedics on board. They had left before the doctor had arrived. They asked me what I had done, and I told them. We got on the helo with Mrs. Reagan and headed straight for the Army hospital at Fort Huachuca.

In the meantime, Brian Hunter, the advance agent at the

Wilsons' ranch called the command center in Arizona and notified the off-duty shift leader, Jimmy Carter, as to what had happened. Agent Carter ordered his shift to get to the hospital and to secure it for the arrival of the President. When we arrived, he greeted us and had everything in place. The President was admitted to the hospital and taken for a series of tests.

As we waited, a nurse came up to me and asked, "Do you mind if I take your blood pressure?"

"No, I don't need my blood pressure taken."

Five more minutes passed. "I would really like to take your blood pressure. You don't look good."

"Okay," I said. "You can take it, but you have to promise me after you take it you won't say anything to a doctor."

"Sure. How bad can it be?"

She took my blood pressure. It was 190 over 100. "I'm going to get a doctor right now. You should be in this hospital more than the President."

The doctors tried to convince me to lie down, but I refused. When the President was declared free to go several hours later, they insisted that I stay to monitor my blood pressure. Again I refused, telling them that I knew my blood pressure would be high after the stressful events of the day.

We returned later that day to Bill Wilson's ranch with a male nurse attending to the President. We continued on with the ranch visit. However, there was no more horseback riding. One month later, the President started to complain that his head was bothering him. The doctors at the Mayo Clinic discovered a blood clot in his brain, which had perhaps been caused by the fall. He had surgery, which required them to drill a hole through his skull to remove the clot.

7

The Assassination Attempt

Our job in the Secret Service is to always be thinking about how The Jackal might try to harm the president. It was a cool afternoon on March 30, 1981, when The Jackal in the form of John Hinckley, Jr., almost succeeded in killing the President.

When the shooting happened, I was just getting off duty and leaving the White House. Moments earlier, I had been with Mrs. Reagan at a luncheon in Washington, D.C. She had initially planned to accompany her husband to the Washington Hilton that afternoon. At the last minute, her chief of staff, Elaine Crispin, encouraged her to accept an invitation to a luncheon at the Georgetown home of Michael Ainsley, president of the National Trust for Historic Preservation. For some reason, Mrs. Reagan felt that she needed to leave early and return to the White House, sensing something was going to happen.

Returning from the luncheon, Mrs. Reagan entered the White House from the south grounds and walked through the Diplomatic Room and onto the private elevator up to the solarium.

Word of the shooting reached the agents at "staircase," the code word for the family detail command post inside the presidential mansion. The first reports that came over the Secret Service radio communicated that there had been a shooting, but that the President was okay. He was being whisked back to the White House for security reasons. Mrs. Reagan's security detail leader, George Opfer, went to the solarium and signaled her to come out. This was unusual.

Clearly concerned, Mrs. Reagan looked both puzzled and worried. They entered the elevator, and on the way down George told her what had happened. Soon after the initial reports, however, information was released saying that the presidential limousine was indeed going to the hospital. Mrs. Reagan was now very concerned and said, "If he isn't hurt, why are they going to the hospital?" It was a good question, but we didn't know the answer to it.

She said to George, "Take me to the hospital."

"Mrs. Reagan, we are not sure what's going on," George told her. "We'd rather you stay here at the White House."

"Either you take me, or I'll walk." George called her car up and took her to the hospital.

When I heard her say that, I thought, *Good for you*. Sometime later, I told her so.

I found out from some of the other agents that Jerry Parr was in the back of the limo with the President, and Drew Unrue was the driver. Ray Shaddick was the shift leader and sat in the front seat working the radios. It was Jerry who pushed the President into the limo after the shots were fired. All agents are trained in first aid and advanced medical procedures. Once they were both in the limo, Jerry immediately examined the President, running his hands over him to see if he was all right. As Drew tore off at a high speed, the President kept saying, "I'm not hit, I'm not hit, Jerry." Yet, shots had been fired, and Jerry was hearing over his radio that agent Tim McCarthy had been hit while doing his job protecting the President. He also heard that civilians were down. Those of us who weren't with the President were now worried that he was injured and that another follow-up attack might be imminent. Was the Hinckley shooting just a diversion?

Drew had orders to turn onto Constitution Avenue and make his way back to the White House. Agents who drive these armored limos are specially trained out of the Transportation Section (TS). They know the routes to the White House better than anyone else knows, and Drew was following the route perfectly. In the backseat, the President said in a weak voice, "Jerry, I'm not hit but my ribs are sore. I think you might have broken my rib when you threw me in the car." The President had hit the transmission hump when he landed.

Jerry kept asking, "Are you feeling anything?"

Then, just as Drew was approaching the final checkpoint where the decision had to be made if he would proceed to the White House or the hospital, the President coughed and blood came out of the corner of his mouth. It was like red coffee grounds. From the medical training he had received, Jerry knew this meant a lung injury, because the air was causing the bubbles that looked like coffee grounds.

Jerry now ordered, "Take us to the hospital!"

Drew had just taken the route that committed them to the White House, so he turned the wheel hard—and *whoosh!*— that huge and very heavy armored limo took a sharp turn and sped toward George Washington University Hospital.

Every time a president goes anywhere, the Secret Service sets up a designated hospital in advance. We conduct a hospital survey to check if it has a burn center, a fully staffed emergency room, orthopedic surgeons, neurologists, and any other specialist there may be. We also request that these doctors be available or on immediate standby, even if it is a Sunday or their day off. A phone is installed in the hospital, and an agent sits right next to it the entire time the president is in the area. If that phone rings, it is that agent's task to set everything in motion and to do it fast. Usually, the job is very boring, but if and when that phone rings, it is pure chaos. Fear and adrenaline kick in and take over.

Drew knew right where to go. The limo went screaming up Pennsylvania Avenue. When he pulled into the emergency room entrance, everything was already in place. The doctors were waiting for him, and the orderlies were lined up. The agent at the hospital had worked at breakneck speed to put everything in place. This was a busy hospital, and there had been ambulances at that entrance only minutes earlier. Needing to clear the area, the agent had grabbed some police officers and shouted at them, "Get these people out of here and clear the area. The President's limo is coming in."

When the limo pulled up, Ray jumped out of the front, and Jerry bailed out of the back. They helped the President out, taking him by the elbows. "I'm okay," he told them. He then took just two steps and collapsed. Jerry and Ray were trying to hold him up when the hospital staff in white coats came running with a gurney for him.

Mrs. Reagan arrived at the hospital shortly afterwards. It was Michael Deaver who met her in the hallway and told her that her husband had been shot. This was the first time she had heard this, and she went white. "I want to see him," she said. The hospital staff explained to her that he was undergoing tests, and it would be best if she did not see him until he was finished. Mrs. Reagan was taken to a small room, where her friend Senator Paul Laxalt joined her.

Finally, she was escorted to her husband's side. She held his hand. His mouth was covered with blood. That's when he said, "Honey, I forgot to duck."

They cut off his new suit, and he was stabilized. The X-rays revealed the flattened bullet, and the doctors rushed him into the operating room, accompanied by Jerry Parr, who remained with him throughout the surgery.

The attempt on the President's life revealed to the nation his raw physical courage. It also demonstrated Mrs. Reagan's incredible emotional strength. This woman was small in size but huge in courage. She sat by her husband's side almost continuously to help him overcome this great challenge both he and the country now faced, and she did it without flinching once.

The Secret Service trains and trains to make sure something like this never happens. So what went wrong? The reality is, no security system is perfect. The only way to make sure that the president is completely protected is to dig a bunker and keep him there. There are always risks—while often very small—of a terrorist attack or a gunman like Hinckley.

On that day, several circumstances played out.

Wherever the President goes, the news media go, recording his every movement. On this afternoon, it was no different outside the Washington Hilton. Reagan was speaking to a crowd of AFL-CIO union delegates. The news media were inside covering the event. Also, across the street from the hotel, a cluster of mostly press photographers had gathered where they thought the President might be exiting. We now know that Hinckley was standing with them with his gun in his belt. Although he didn't know exactly when the President was going to exit the Hilton that afternoon, he had, nonetheless, been stalking him.

He walked right into the group of the assembled press corps. All the members of the media usually wear special tags, and normally there would have been an area cordoned off for them and monitored by an assigned agent. However, this was just a small, informal group attempting to film his departure. The news media are usually mindful of who is with them. If they had noticed a suspicious person like Hinckley with no press credentials, they would have notified us, but no one said anything.

When the President emerged from the hotel, the news media photographers across the street started yelling his name, wanting him to look their way. The President, jovial as he always was, heard them and waved back. At this point, the press rushed across the street, and Hinckley moved with them. He positioned himself in the front row as they gathered near the President. He pulled the weapon out and placed it directly over the shoulder of D.C. police officer Delehanty.

Hinckley fired five or six rounds in less than two seconds: bang, bang, bang, bang, bang. That was all it took.

People often ask me, why did he use a .22? Because it's a small caliber weapon, and when they can get close in like that, professional assassins use the type of .22 he did. Unlike a .357, which would blow a hole in you and then exit your body, a .22 has high velocity, and when it hits you it starts ricocheting off everything inside—muscles, bones, and major organs. It grinds you up and eats you up inside. So a .22 was, unfortunately, the perfect assassin's weapon in this situation. The type of round Hinckley used is called a devastator because it is made to have an explosive charge that goes off when it hits its target. Only providence and a great medical team saw to it that Reagan survived.

The round that hit the President had first ricocheted off the armored limo's glass. (The limo's rear double doors swung backwards.) We were lucky. If the doors had opened like a conventional car, he would have been hit with the bullet's full force, but the damage was still life threatening. When the round entered the President under his left armpit, it had been flattened to approximately the size of a dime and was razor sharp.

Like everyone else, I spent most of the day watching television, waiting anxiously for the next news report. I did call the White House, offering to return to work if they needed more manpower at the hospital. I was thinking, *Are we going to lose this great man just three months into his presidency?* If Jerry had not ordered the vehicle to go to the hospital instead of the White House, the President would have surely died.

Some people have said that after the assassination attempt, Reagan was a different man. One change was the President's resolve about dealing with the Soviet Union. He saw a divine purpose behind his surviving the assassin's bullet. He resolutely believed that God had spared his life to give him time to defeat communism. Just one month later, when Pope John Paul II survived an attack, it became even more clear to him.

BEING THE MOST powerful man in the world is something that must be difficult for even the president himself to grasp—the benefits, the responsibilities, and the burdens he has inherited while he is sitting in the Oval Office. He does understand that he is on the world's stage, and because of that, when it comes to his safety, it is reassuring for him to look out and see some friendly, recognizable faces.

President Reagan liked and respected the Secret Service agents. At the same time, the agents had a love for the Reagans. Agents are willing to give their lives for any president. That is quite simply our job, but with the Reagans, there was a special bond.

The bridge between the First Couple and me was built early on. While Mrs. Reagan was always courteous to all the agents, she really knew me after I caught her falling off her horse. From that point on, she associated me with safety and someone whom the President felt very comfortable with. It was, however, only a few years later that I found myself entangled in a difficult situation. By 1984, I had been on PPD for six years. The normal term is three to four years, and for me, it had gotten to the point where I wanted to leave and continue with my career and get back to criminal work. I called Joe Carlon, who was the assistant director of investigations of the Secret Service and who had also been my Counterfeit Squad leader when I was still in Boston in the 1970s.

"What do you want?" he asked me.

"I want the Arizona office."

He turned on the computer and then said, "You've got it." It was quite a feat just to get something like that. What helped me was that I had worked under him in Boston, and I took directions very well. He remembered that.

There was just one problem. Joe failed to notify the Arizona office and explain the situation. Surprised, some of the agents got nervous when they heard that Barletta was coming. Often, when there are orders for someone new to take over an office, they transfer the current supervisor in that office. Joe eased their concerns when he explained why I was coming.

I had only four months to sell or rent my house in Arlington, Virginia, and find a new one in Arizona. Having gone to college in Arizona, I knew that was somewhere I would like to live. I made a few phone calls and quickly put into motion the process necessary to get moved within 120 days. I even made all the arrangements to send my horse Ruler of the Roost to Arizona by truck and to have him taken care of when he arrived there. That was not something the Secret Service would pay for.

It didn't take long for the President to find out about this, and one day, when we were out riding, he asked, "I understand you're going to be leaving us?"

"Yes, sir."

"Is it something we've done?"

"Sir, of course not."

"Well, then, what do you want?"

"Because of the circumstances, I need to move on," I tried to explain. "The Secret Service tells me that I need to master other skills if I want to get ahead and receive promotions. This is what I need to do if I want to further my career."

He then asked, "What does John Barletta really want to do?"

"I want to do what the Secret Service tells me to do." I was beating around the bush, and he knew it. We just kept riding, and that was the end of our discussion about it.

That summer, I was assigned to the advance work for the Republican Convention in Dallas. It was a huge responsibility. While I was in Dallas, the command post called to tell me that John Simpson, the director of the U.S. Secret Service, wanted to see me up in his hotel suite. I headed right up there, figuring he wanted to be briefed about something. Director Simpson and I were both from Boston, and I had previously worked with his brother who was a Boston Metropolitan police officer. When I arrived at his suite, he said, "John, I'm canceling your transfer."

Shocked, I asked, "What?"

"I'm canceling your transfer. You're not going, you're staying here."

"Sir, you know how things normally work. I should be leaving PPD for something else."

"Yes, but you're in a very extraordinary circumstance, and I want you to stay right here where you are. You can move to Arizona and be in charge of that office. I know you would accomplish a lot, but that doesn't mean anything compared with keeping the President safe. What you're doing is extremely more important. I want you here."

"Sir," I said, "I'm just about ready to sign on a house. I'll lose the deposit, and I've already rented my house out in Arlington. I've spent money. My horse is on the road as we speak."

He said, "Well, just put in a voucher and you'll be reimbursed."

"You cannot voucher transportation of pets, and a horse is considered a pet. It's costing me three thousand dollars to ship him out West."

He was making it clear that the decision had been made. "You put it in a voucher, and it will *all* be approved."

"May I ask why this is going on?"

He just said, "No. See you later." He had me promoted, and I stayed.

Years later, I found out that the President had been involved in the matter. During that period, he had been talking to Barney and Dennis out at the ranch about my transfer. Finally, they asked the President, "What do you think?"

"Well, I think John should stay here. I feel safer with him around." To this day, I believe he said that because of the bond between us that began with the horses. Obviously, I did not accomplish keeping the President safe alone—many dedicated, hardworking agents accomplished it. The reason he wanted me to stay was not that I was a superior agent but that he felt comfortable with me. Having me nearby was important to him. We had become close because of our mutual love of horses and the time we had spent together.

When Director Simpson heard what the President had said, he canceled my transfer orders, but I didn't find that out for a long time.

8

With World Leaders

While most of the time the ranch was a secluded retreat for Reagan and the First Lady, on rare occasions he would invite a foreign leader with whom he would share the beautiful vistas. I think he believed that if his special guests could see the place he loved most, they would come to understand him even better, and in turn, would trust him more. I think he knew its simple beauty would impress them.

When foreign leaders such as Gorbachev and Queen Elizabeth visited, they were amazed at the simplicity of the place. No doubt they were expecting a ranch like the Ewings had on the television show *Dallas*, a massive edifice with white columns, oversized windows, and luxurious furniture. What they got instead, however, was a small adobe house with two bedrooms and some wicker furniture.

Gorbachev's visit to Rancho del Cielo in 1992 made history. Who could have imagined even seven years earlier that these two Cold War adversaries would be meeting at the Reagan Ranch? Gorbachev had only recently resigned as general secretary of the Soviet Union, which had ceased to exist.

Although the Secret Service needed to prepare for this unprecedented visit, the actual process wasn't very complex. The Dignitary Protective Division (DPD) assigns supervisors and agents from all around the country to protect a head of state who has been officially invited to the United States. Now when we travel to Russia, China, or wherever, the Secret Service protects our president no matter where he goes, but here, we accommodate foreign heads of state, and they ride in our vehicles with us. We're protecting them, and they know that. Furthermore, we can do it better than anybody else can, and they know that too. Except for a few of the agents that they send along, they're almost completely under our care.

Because Reagan and Gorbachev had held four summit meetings in the 1980s, we had gotten to know Gorbachev's people, including the members of the KGB who traveled with him and protected him. While they were traveling in the United States with the Secret Service in preparation for the 1987 summit meeting in Washington, D.C., the KBG agents gradually began to trust us with providing protection for their leader. The more we knew, the better we could protect him. They started to entrust us with some of their key information, and it was then that they began to realize that we were not a threat. The deep roots of their mistrust of Americans were embedded in the way they were brought up. However, as we dealt with them, both in their country and in ours, we learned to get along. When we sat down and had a glass of vodka with them and talked one-on-one, we could usually make out okay.

The KGB could be tough, but they were also willing to work with us. During the 1988 visit the Reagans made to Moscow we ran into a serious problem. Mrs. Reagan was waiting for her

hairdresser, Julius Bengston, but he didn't show up. We made
some inquiries and finally discovered that the KGB had arrested
him! They didn't think he was a spy, but he'd been caught trying
to buy goods on the black market on a street in Moscow with
U.S. currency, and he didn't have his passport with him. They
were holding him in a jail cell. I went to see Mrs. Reagan and
told her.

"What?!"

"He's in jail for trafficking foreign currency on the black
market. That's a serious offense in Russia."

"What is going to happen?" she asked.

"The State Department is working on it. He'll be out of
there before dinner—I'm pretty sure."

We had warned White House staff about doing that sort of
thing, but he had ignored what we said. After making a few
phone calls, we did manage to get him released.

These were the waning days of the Cold War, so there was
still some distrust. When we were in the Soviet Union during the
1980s, the CIA would brief everyone traveling with or for the
President, including the ambassadors. Every time we entered the
country they told us, "Act as if you're being tape recorded no
matter where you go, because most of the time you are." During
one extended trip, a few fellow agents and I were just sitting in
my room and talking when I claimed to know some things about
Russia—something to do with the military. Although I was just
kidding around, it caused quite a stir because we were being
taped, and the Soviets took it seriously.

When the CIA found this out, they made it clear to us that
they did not think it was too funny, but the Soviets were reluc-

tant to press the issue any further because they would be forced to admit that they had been taping us. Instead, they claimed that they had discovered the information through other channels, from other intelligence agencies. The CIA saw problems with that and did not believe them. When they found out it was me, it was dropped.

Distrust was one problem with the KGB, temptation was another. When new KGB agents arrived in the United States, they were briefed because the Soviet leadership always had to consider that an agent might defect once he saw our way of life. They always wanted to shop to get some American goods—some to keep, some to sell on the black market. It was overwhelming for them to see all that we had. If you took them into a department store, they would go crazy. One department store in Los Angeles had more merchandise than there was in an entire city in Russia.

President Reagan once told me a great story about the Soviet Union. One day there was a Russian who needed his plumbing fixed. When he called and explained his problem, they told him there would be a ten-year wait before he could get it fixed. The Russian asked, "What time will you be coming?"

"What difference does it make? That's ten years from now," the plumber responded.

"Yes, but the electrician's coming that day too."

For these agents, to even see cars with different colors was something. They had black, and then they had black. The fact that even kids were driving cars amazed them. They were also shocked that in a city there was not one paper, but several. All the churches and the number of people who attended church

surprised them too. They had magnificent, beautiful churches in
Russia, but under communism, the people weren't allowed to go.
They can now, thanks to Ronald Reagan.

Between the protection already at the ranch, the DPD, and
the cooperation of the Soviet agents, security was in place for
the Gorbachevs' visit. We were ready. When Mikhail and Raisa
Gorbachev actually rode up to the property, there were just two
KGB agents with them. The rest stayed at the bottom of the
mountain with the motorcade. The same was true with our
agents. There was no reason for a horde of people to be following them around. Excited to take them on a tour, the first thing
the President showed them was his modest house. You could tell
Gorbachev was more impressed by its simplicity than he would
have been by something grand. Then they strode up the path
that led to the barn. The President was eager to show Gorbachev
his tack room and horses.

When we reached the barn, the two men went into the tack
room. I stayed outside. While leaning against a hitching post, I
noticed the KGB agents were pointing at the gas pump located
near the barn and talking animatedly. Almost every ranch has
its own gas pump because it is extremely difficult to take the
equipment from most ranches to a gas station. You can't drive a
D-4 or a D-9 tractor down a treacherous road to get gas at the
Shell Station. The President had a five thousand–gallon tank,
and once every couple of years a tanker would come up and fill
it. That gas was for all the farm machinery. On the pump were
numbers like fifty cents a gallon, hi test, but they didn't mean
anything.

Now curious, I asked the interpreter, "What are they talking
about? What are they so interested in?"

The interpreter went over to find out. He came back and told me, "The gist of it is, they're amazed that in the United States gasoline is only fifty cents a gallon." They concluded that because of the numbers on the pump.

I started to explain it to him, but then I thought, you know what, I'm just going to let them think that.

The President took his time showing the Gorbachevs around. To give Gorbachev a better view of the ranch, he took him for a ride in his blue Jeep with the GIPPER license plate. That was fun for the President. After their ride together, we strolled back down to the residence where the news media were waiting. That was just one of the few times they were allowed to be on the ranch. They asked questions, all through an interpreter, like, "How did the visit go, Mr. Gorbachev? What do you think of the ranch?"

Members of the news media were all huddled together outside the fence the President had built out of telephone poles, while he leaned against his fence on the inside. At one point during the news media visit, the President handed Gorbachev a beautiful Stetson silver belly cowboy hat. The Soviet premier took it and put it on his head. It's called the Cattlemen's model, and the brim is very flat as compared with a cowboy hat with a more pronounced brim. Unless you really know a lot about cowboy hats, you wouldn't have realized that he had put it on backwards. I said to one of the staff members, "It's on backwards."

"What's on backwards?" he asked me.

"The cowboy hat is on backwards."

"Well, tell him."

"I'm not going to tell the former leader of the Soviet Union that his hat's on backwards. That's not in my job description."

The next day when the President came to the tack room, he looked at me the moment he walked in and said, "It was on backwards, wasn't it?"

"Yes it was, sir, but you know what? No one's going to know." The President said that he had tried to tell him, but Gorbachev did not speak English, and the President didn't want to go through the interpreter. He didn't want to take the chance of embarrassing the Soviet premier in front of the news media. So he just let it go. President Reagan was always thoughtful, handling everything with grace. He would never want to embarrass anyone.

Margaret Thatcher was another one of the rare guests to visit the ranch. She and the President were very good friends. He called her Maggie and she called him Ronnie. Other than Mrs. Reagan, she was the only person who called him Ronnie. I think it was our support of the British during the Falkland Islands crisis that sealed their relationship. During the ordeal, President Reagan called Mrs. Thatcher to tell her that if the United States could do anything for them, just let him know. She was a very forceful and mission-orientated woman and a deep thinker, yet at the same time, she was a very pleasant woman. Her husband, Dennis Thatcher, was also a nice, intelligent, unassuming guy who was in a somewhat difficult situation, a role reversal in a sense.

During the Thatchers' visit, they went inside the tack room. There on the wall was a poster that was a parody of the famous promotional shot for *Gone With the Wind* where Clark Gable is passionately holding Vivian Leigh in his arms. Someone had superimposed President Reagan's head on Gable's body and Mrs. Thatcher's on Leigh's. Instead of a picture of Atlanta burning in the background, on this poster there was a drawing of a bomb going off with the words "Together we can do this." Mr. Thatcher got a kick out of that. He had a good sense of humor.

When the queen of England came in 1983, we had torrential rains. We'd go for years with no rain at the ranch, but that year we had monsoons. The Queen had sailed in on her ship *Britannia*. It was Mrs. Reagan's birthday, and she wanted to take the First Lady out on her royal yacht for a cruise. The *Britannia* was huge, but the seas were so bad that even it couldn't get into the Santa Barbara harbors. The captain finally had to navigate the ship down to Los Angeles where Mrs. Reagan was taken to board the ship.

To transport Queen Elizabeth and Prince Philip safely to the ranch, we had to drive them in a Chevy Suburban. We needed a vehicle capable of high clearance over those crossings where the water was raging. An armored limo might have had a problem going through those areas. Unfortunately, a woman in a Volkswagen was washed away trying to traverse those very crossings.

When they arrived at the ranch, it was still pouring rain. However, the staff was really pressuring the President and the Queen to get on horses, since he had ridden with her at Windsor Castle a year earlier. The English are superb riders. They have the best foxhunting in the world, and they discovered polo centuries ago in India. I have high respect for their riding abilities. However, I said, "Take a look at those holes. Those are gopher holes. You see the water bubbling up? This ranch is saturated. They're going to sink out there. They cannot ride, period. The President knows that, and the Queen knows that. Yes, it's disappointing. It would have been a great photo opportunity."

In the end, they didn't ride, and I was glad they didn't. The Queen had these magnificent, spit-shined creatures, while the

President had ranch horses with nicks on them. They were not groomed every day by any means. Hay was thrown out under a tree for them, not ground oats. The difference was unbelievable. The Queen would have loved it and would have handled it fine, because she's a gracious lady. The President would've been totally at ease too, because he didn't care if he was on a magnificent looking creature or his ranch horse. To him, a good horse was a good horse. If for some reason she didn't like his ranch horse, he would've just thought, *There's nothing I can do about it.*

Mrs. Reagan was very apologetic about the rain. There's a picture of the Queen with her babushka and raincoat on, still looking regal, standing next to Mrs. Reagan. The Queen touched her and graciously said, "That's okay, my dear, it makes me feel at home. It's exciting. This is an adventure." There was talk about canceling the ranch visit because of the weather, but the Queen wouldn't hear of that. She had to see the ranch. Before they left, they all had lunch.

A YEAR BEFORE Queen Elizabeth's visit to the ranch, the President traveled to Great Britain where he went horseback riding on the grounds of Windsor Castle. To prepare for his trip to the Queen's castle, my boss Will Slade and I, along with some other staff members, flew over in advance. The main purpose of our trip was to have everything ready for the President's ride with the Queen. While there were plenty of agents taking care of all the other details, any agent covering the riding part of the trip had to be well informed about horses. The level of preparation for such a trip is mind-boggling. Months before we arrived, the State Department had been working in tandem with the British authorities and the Queen's staff.

On our arrival, Will and I immediately went to the Queen's stables on the grounds of Windsor Castle. Everything was impeccable—the grounds, the buildings, and the stables. I was struck by how nice it was. When we entered the stables, the first person we saw was Sir John, who was in charge of all the Queen's equestrian needs. An older rigid-looking fellow, he stood straight as an arrow. Just by looking at him, you could tell he was a heck of a rider without ever seeing him on a horse. He was in charge of everything equestrian—the tack room, the horses, and the carriages—everything. Sir John introduced himself to us. He was knighted, and he carried himself in such a manner.

I explained to Sir John that I needed to see the horse the President was going to ride. I also needed to check out the course the President would take with the Queen. Sir John showed me the magnificent thoroughbred that had been selected for the President. Centennial was big, sixteen to seventeen hands high, easily. I said, "I'd like to ride him."

"No one sits astride the Queen's horse," he told me.

I persisted, "Sir John, I was told that you were informed about just what was going to happen, that you were going to show me where the Queen and the President are going to ride. It will be a huge benefit for us all considering your expertise. We are counting on that."

"No, you can't ride that horse."

Realizing this was going nowhere, I said, "Well, okay. This is my job, but you're the boss." All the stable hands were watching our exchange.

I marched out of the stalls and went straight to our embassy to report what had just happened. Our embassy notified the State Department at once. The State Department then fired back at the

British Embassy, which went directly to the Queen's staff, which finally reached Sir John. The message was clear: if John Barletta doesn't ride the Queen's horse, the President won't ride it.

Well, now he's lost face, and he's steaming mad at me. Will and I headed back to the stables the next day dressed in jeans, a polo shirt, a baseball cap, and Dehner boots. When we entered, Sir John looked at us as if we were a couple of lost cowboys. Pleasantly I said, "Sir John, I know they called you. I hope there are no ill feelings involved here. This is my job. The President would just feel more comfortable if I had been on the horse before him. I know the horse is magnificent. I know there's nothing wrong with him, but I want to be able to give the President some hints such as, sir, don't pull on him too much, give him plenty of rein, and don't touch him with your spurs. He wants that information before he mounts Centennial, because he wants to ride the Queen's horse the way the horse is used to being ridden."

Knowing that he now had no other choice, he said, "Well, okay," but he wasn't happy.

I had already contacted the grooms, since they were the ones responsible for getting the horses ready. I wanted to be on their good side. Whatever I said must have worked, because Centennial was already tacked up when Will and I arrived that morning. "Sir John," I asked, "will the horse be tacked up when the President and the Queen arrive?"

With a hint of sarcasm in his voice that I would even ask such a question, he said, "Of course."

"Well, you know, the President tacks up his own horse."

"Oh, he does?" I'm sure he was thinking, *You Americans really are different.*

Will and I mounted our horses and off we went with Sir John. "Just show us where we're going to go," I said. "We don't have to ride the whole course. I just want to see the terrain. I hope we're not going to jump anything during the President's ride, but if we are, I need to know in advance."

"No. There'll be no jumping."

"Good, good," I said.

Once we were out on the course, Sir John picked up the pace. He was testing us. That was typical. That was acceptable, and I understood. Then we started running, and now there were three powerful horses running. That was dangerous if you don't know what you're doing, and sometimes even if you do. Will was a great rider, better than I was, and Sir John had more knowledge in his little finger about horses than I'll ever have in my whole lifetime. Looking ahead, I saw that we were approaching a water crossing, and I thought, *Are we going to hit that water at a run?* You just don't hit a stream with a running horse unless you have to. That's usually done only in the movies. I looked over at Will and asked, "Is he going to hit that stream at full run? If he does, we are too."

In an instant, we all hit the water together, but Sir John's horse stumbled, and he fell off. The horse didn't bolt or anything, he just went down. This was November, and Sir John was sprawled out in the icy water. Thoroughbreds don't stop easily, and by the time I got Centennial stopped and Will had stopped his horse, we'd both ridden quite a distance past the water. Wanting to give some aid to Sir John, we turned around, rode back to the water crossing, and jumped off our horses. His body wasn't hurt, but his pride was.

He was really mad now, and I knew he was thinking, *Those*

damn Americans. The fact is, we shouldn't have been running in the first place, and we definitely shouldn't have been running hitting that water. He knew it, and I knew it. He was just trying to prove a point the wrong way.

Not exactly sure what to do next, I said, "There's no reason to continue." We were all ready to get back to the stables, and Sir John was cold and soaking wet. When we finally brought the horses back in, his helpers knew that he had fallen because he was all wet. For Sir John, that was even more degrading to him than coming off his horse.

As we dismounted I said, "Sir John, I can't apologize enough. Thank you so much for doing this. I will inform our President, and I will tell him how helpful you were. Are you sure you're all right?"

"I'm all right." He was a man of unbending strength. I thought he had to be in his seventies.

Next I asked, "What will the dress be?"

"Oh, that's okay. What you're wearing right now will be fine." Well, remember, we were dressed in jeans, polo shirts, baseball caps, windbreakers, and Dehner boots. The boots were the only things we were wearing that were proper dress for the ride. Obviously what we had on wouldn't be fine for a ride with the Queen. During the short time we had been in the stables, I had befriended one of the stable hands. He told me Sir John thought we were just a couple of American cowboys who would never ride English—thinking we'd probably come in with our lassoes. I said to the boy, "He's trying to set us up again. You don't ride with the Queen wearing jeans."

"No," he said. "They'll be all dressed up."

In preparation for our trip to England, I had told the boys to bring dark tweed sports jackets, English pants, ascots, and boots that were so polished you would be able to shave by looking at them. Dressed to the nines, we arrived all decked out on the day of the ride. When Sir John and I saw each other, I just said, "*Nice outfit*, sir."

Before anyone else arrived, Sir John informed me, "Now, when the Queen comes, you don't talk to her or Prince Philip."

"What do you mean?"

"Well, the protocol is you don't talk to them."

"Okay, thank you for telling us that. We could have made a huge *faux pas* here, and I would have been embarrassed, since I don't know your customs 100 percent. I really appreciate your help. Now we're working together."

The time finally came for the Queen, the Prince, and the First Couple to arrive. Both the Queen and the Prince are consummate horse people. My first impression of them was how grand they looked. The President was all decked out too. Standing in a big circle, the Queen introduced Sir John to the President and Mrs. Reagan. "Sir John," she said, "takes care of all my equestrian needs and equipment. He is in charge of everything and does a magnificent job."

Sir John respectfully greeted the First Couple. "How do you do, Mr. President? It's a pleasure to meet you, Mrs. Reagan."

"Thank you," Mrs. Reagan said. Then looking at me she said, "Now that's our John. He is in the Secret Service, and he takes care of all our equestrian needs too."

Prince Philip then said, "Oh, does he?" Looking directly at me, he asked, "What kind of saddles do you use?" I didn't say a word. Things suddenly got very awkward. Still looking at me, he asked, "What kind of horses does the President have at the ranch?"

I slowly turned to Sir John and asked, "Is it okay to talk to him now?"

Later I asked the President, "Did you have a nice ride, sir?"

"Very much," he told me. It was a delightful day for the Reagans.

During the visit, Prince Philip took Mrs. Reagan on an open carriage ride. The Prince had been a phenomenal polo player, even competing in the Summer Olympics. Polo players are tough, and they know how to ride. They almost become a part of their horse. As he got older, however, he could no longer compete, so he started competitive carriage driving. In fact, he introduced carriage driving into the Olympics, where they go through an unbelievable obstacle course. The Prince could maneuver his two-horse carriage into places I couldn't put my car. He was fantastic.

I went on the carriage ride, hopping inside and sitting directly behind the First Lady. Prince Philip was seated on the right side, and behind him was a young lad dressed in a black suit, a black bollo hat, and an ascot. Holding his whip, the Prince soon had us going at a good speed. His two horses were pulling the carriage quickly over the cobblestones when I noticed that there was an intersection ahead. I could hardly believe what I saw next. There was a bar attached to the carriage on the driver's side. Before we arrived at the intersection, the Prince slowed down slightly while this young man jumped out of the carriage and ran ahead of the horses and into the intersection. He held his arm out to stop any potential traffic so that the Prince wouldn't have to slow down.

When we started passing by the young man, the horses trotting through the intersection, he put his arm out and wrapped it around the bar and jumped back into the carriage. We were still going at a good speed when Mrs. Reagan turned around and just looked at me, her eyes wide. "I hope you don't think I'm gonna do that," I said to her.

She laughed and said, "No, but I am astonished."

As we started going over a bridge, the Prince asked, "I suppose you people have someone under my bridge, in the water too?"

"Yes we do, sir," I answered. "We've got the Navy frogmen." The British are not accustomed to the heavy protection we have for our leaders. They do not like all that security. I think they view our country as a bunch of cowboys where everybody carries a gun.

After the ride, Mrs. Reagan pulled me aside and asked, "Do we really have people under that water?"

"Yes, ma'am, we do."

In the late 1980s, George Chamberlin, a rancher from the Santa Ynez Valley, invited Sir John to his ranch. Sir John had hosted George when he had visited England earlier. In honor of Sir John's visit to California, George held a dinner party to which I was coincidentally invited. George asked me if I knew him, and I said, "Oh, yes, and I think he will remember me too." The night of the party, Sir John and I greeted each other and exchanged cordial pleasantries.

Just recently, a friend of mine returned from England who

had spoken with Sir John while he was there. During their conversation, Sir John, who is now in his nineties, referred to the impertinent, cowboy Secret Service agent. As soon as my friend heard that, he thought, *He must be talking about John Barletta.*

THE RELATIONSHIP between Pope John Paul II and the Reagans was special. They hit it off immediately. The Pope never chastised the President about his decisions, but he was concerned about all people in every country. Although they used different methods, these were two men willing to confront the evils of the world. He'd say, "Mr. President, you have to make peace. You have to do this for the world."

"I'm trying, Your Holiness, I'm trying," the President would say in a way that would reassure him. The Pope liked Mrs. Reagan too. That was evident by his expressions in the pictures taken of them together.

On one occasion, we went to the Pope's summer residence. Nobody goes there. I mean nobody. I once invited a priest to my home, and when I told him about my trip to the Pope's summer home, he asked in amazement, "You met the Pope? You were at his summer residence?" I showed him the picture.

The threat of assassination against the Pope is greater than against anyone else in the world because of what he symbolizes to all the fanatics that would like to kill him. When he visits the United States, he receives even more protection than the president does. Due to the level of the threats against his life, the preparations for his travels are extremely challenging. Wherever he goes, the Pope travels in the Popemobile. The vehicle with the glass bubble-shaped top that he has used ever since he was shot at in 1981. Although it is completely bulletproof, it is constructed out of glass because he refused to use such a secured vehicle unless he could see all the people and wave at them.

It was exhausting to work on the Pope's detail. We used to call that vehicle the "Poopmobile" because we were all pooped out from working so long running beside it. His aides, who all look like heavyweight boxers, are actually priests. These priests are his version of the Secret Service. They are extremely astute about what it takes to protect someone.

We actually rode in the Popemobile when we traveled to his summer residence. Castelgandolfo, as it is called, is situated on a hill, near the top of an extinct volcano, overlooking a beautiful lake. In a remote spot about twenty miles southeast of Rome, it has been the summer residence of the popes for almost four hundred years. The structure is made of beautiful stone, and from the balcony we took in spectacular views of the Italian countryside.

When we finally arrived at the residence, a decision had to be made as to who was going to go inside. I decided to ask, "Who's Catholic?" I didn't know how else to deal with the situation. Fortunately, everybody agreed with that idea. The priests came out to greet us, and one of them instructed us as to exactly what the Pope was going to do. "He's going to come out and shake everybody's hand. Then he's going to bless you." *Oh that's wonderful*, I thought. I had loaded my pockets with rosary beads because in the Catholic faith, if the Pope blesses you, he's blessing everything on you. I gave one rosary to my mother and my father and kept another for myself.

When I met the Pope I wanted to kneel down, since that is what you do when you meet him, but I didn't. Instead, I kissed his hand and his ring. He was a sweet, humble man, so gracious to all of us. During the past twenty-five years, the world has witnessed his enduring courage and intellect.

He speaks many languages fluently with little or no accent. Not needing a translator, his discussions with the President were held mostly in private. They would just sit and talk for hours. Their visits together began early on during Reagan's presidency. In fact, after the President had been shot, one of his first trips was to visit the Pope. He told him, "I feel like God has given me a warning, and for whatever I do, whatever I accomplish, I owe it to Him. From this day on, my time belongs to God."

9

The Simple Man

President Reagan often told me that being President was a great gift to him *from* the American people. That is how he lived during those eight years of his presidency—it was something wonderful he had received, and he cherished it. He would call the White House public housing. "I'm just living there for a while," he would tell me. People who watched the Reagans during their White House years talk about how they returned grandeur and grace to the Oval Office. All of that is certainly true, but this was a man without an ego, who even as the leader of the Free World was most happy being "Ron."

One rainy day at the ranch, the agents who would otherwise be out riding were all in the tack room just cleaning up some of the equipment. I walked over to talk with everyone for a bit, near where the President was also busy cleaning up some things. The tack room was in a sense the epitome of Reagan's life—hard work, love of the outdoors, simplicity, and attention to basic details. There were peanut butter jars full of bolts and screws, and in boxes, there were hundreds of pieces of leather just in case you might have to fix a cinch or something else. Although the President was generous, he never threw away anything that might still be useful.

One of the agents, Ron Bodenheimer, was on post. He was not a rider, but he had come into the barn with the President. When you were on post, that is what you were supposed to do. Anyway, I wanted something from Ron and called over to him, "Hey, Ron, can you come here a minute?" Well, the President came over, and trying to conceal my shock I calmly said, "No, not you, sir. I would never call you Ron. Not you, sir."

He just said, "Well . . ." It was amazing. In his mind, he was just plain Ron.

He didn't need or even really care for all the pomp and circumstance of the office. President Reagan was often called the "Great Communicator." While he was known for beautiful words and soaring speeches, ordinarily he spoke in very simple words—words everyone could understand. "Plain talk is the way I like it, and plain talk is the way they do it out West," he would say. Still, he was always very polite. He never demanded of anyone, "You will do this," and he never told someone, "Your idea is stupid." At all times, he was the consummate gentleman.

He liked people and gave them his full and interested attention when he spoke to them. His critics complained that he was standoffish. That wasn't true. He just wasn't the kind of person who'd vigorously shake your hand and say have a nice day. Nor would he really put his arm around you. He just didn't do that, but it didn't mean he didn't care about someone. What you saw is what you got. He was just a good person.

President Reagan had bedrock principles that he would die for. One of those was to stand tall in adversity. There was the horrific tragedy in Beirut in 1983. U.S. Marines based in Lebanon were the victims of a truck bomb. Days later, the bodies of 241 Marines returned to Andrews Air Force Base in coffins. The coffins were lined up at the front of the hangar with United States flags draped over each one. All the relatives—the wives, husbands, mothers, fathers, and children—had gathered there to receive their loved ones' bodies and to honor them. It was a difficult, trying situation, and I privately wondered why the President wanted to bring all this on himself. He didn't need to do it, but he wanted to, for the families.

Before the service, I walked up the aisle behind the President and First Lady. In the midst of the quietness of that huge, metal building, I could hear sobbing as we passed by the family members on our way to the front. That was a tough moment. The President solemnly passed by the caskets with Mrs. Reagan and then greeted all the family members. "I'm so sorry," he said. That was the most emotional I had ever seen him. That was the closest I'd seen him to breaking down.

As we were receiving the relatives, Mrs. Reagan started to cry. She wasn't carrying a handbag, because she needed to keep her hands free on those occasions. Seeing that she didn't have a handkerchief, I tapped her on the right hand. Instinctively she knew it was me, and I discreetly placed mine in her hand. Nothing was said. That Christmas, I received a gift from her personally. Not wanting to open the gift in front of the other agents, I waited until after I got home. It was a box of white handkerchiefs. She is a wonderful and thoughtful lady.

One day in 1990, my friend Mark Gowing, who I sponsored to be a Ranchero, brought three Secret Service horses back up to the ranch in his truck from Dr. Herthel's clinic in Los Olivos.

They had been at the veterinarian for regular checkups and to receive their shots. I asked, "Do you want to meet the President? He's here."

"Of course," Mark answered.

When we started walking toward the tack barn, I realized that Mark had gotten so nervous that I thought he might throw up. I reassured him that he shouldn't be nervous, because once he met the President, everything would be fine. "Don't worry, Mark. He will put you totally at ease."

Wanting him to be able to have a private moment with the President, I told Mark that after I introduced them, I was going to step back, which I did.

Mark said, "What a beautiful place you have here, Mr. President."

"Would you like to see a little bit more of it?" the President asked.

Mark looked at me astonished, and I said, "Go ahead. You don't need me now." For a few minutes, just the two of them walked around the area near the barn while the President talked to him about the things he had built. The President was genuine, and that memory is one of the fondest of Mark's life.

I recall times when we would be riding in a motorcade when it was raining hard, just pouring. The streets would be lined with people who had turned out just to see the armored limo with the American flag and the Presidential seal crawl by, knowing it was the President who was in that vehicle. The windows are heavily tinted, which prevents the people from actually seeing the President. Still he would be waving to everyone. "Sir," I reminded him, "they can't see you."

"Yes," he said knowingly, "but I want to do this."

Sometimes his thoughtfulness would put me in a tricky situation. When you cover the President, there are five positions you work. If one agent gets out of position because the President turns, everybody switches positions so that hole is filled. You really practice that so it's not like a dance drill but instead just flows. Once we were going through a door, and the number one agent opened it because he was the lead agent. I was on the President's left side, and on his right side there was a female agent. Well, the President stopped at the open door and gave her the gesture to go ahead of him. Perplexed, she looked at me, and I could tell she was thinking, *What do I do? I'm not supposed to go ahead of him. That's not my position.* He was trying to be polite as always, wanting her to go first.

So I jumped in and said, "She's an agent, sir, and she's doing her job. You need to go first."

He just looked at me for a moment and then said, "Yes, I know she is an agent, but she is a lady first."

Now she was sweating, so I told her, "Karen, go through the door." Then he smiled at me and nodded, because that was how he felt it should be.

Presidents don't carry money with them, and after a while they naturally forget to keep track of just what things cost. Often, he would ask me about the price of something because he wanted to be mindful of that. I can clearly recall the time he asked me about the price of hotel rooms. "John, how much does a room cost?"

"Well, sir, it depends where it is located, what city it is in, and the type of room it is."

"How about the room we stayed in last night?"

"That was the Reagan Presidential Suite at the Century Plaza Hotel, and it costs five thousand dollars a night."

"What?!"

Another time he asked me about the price of haircuts. Every two weeks he would go to get a trim. "John, how much is it for a haircut these days?" he asked me.

"Mr. President, that would be twenty-five dollars."

He was always concerned if the barber was receiving a generous tip. "How much should we tip him?"

"Sir, that has already been taken care of."

"Are you sure?"

"Yes, Mr. President." The bills were all sent to and paid by Kay Pieata. The tip had already been added to the account. Still, he would have liked to see the money actually go into the barber's hands. At one point, I told Kay that maybe we should just let him give a tip because it would have felt good to him to put his hand in his pocket and pull out the money. However, that wouldn't have been appropriate for him to do. The President did always carry a couple of lucky coins in his pocket. You could hear them jingle.

There were times when his thoughtfulness lifted spirits. I had told a military aide that my brother Ed was facing a life-threatening, triple bypass operation. The aide, in turn, told the President. One morning soon after Ed's surgery, we were in the tack room readying our equipment when the President asked, "How is your brother Ed doing?"

"He's recuperating in the hospital. The operation was a success," I told him.

"Why don't we give him a call?"

Surprised, I said, "Excuse me, Mr. President?"

"Do you mind if I call your brother?"

"No, sir."

So he picked up the phone and handed it to me. Personnel on the WHCA switchboard knew that it was the President's phone line and answered it, "Yes, Mr. President." I explained who I was and that the President wanted to place a call to my brother. I gave them the number of the Beth Israel Hospital in Boston and his room number. Immediately, they put the call through to the hospital. When the initial call came through, the receptionist at the hospital didn't believe it was a call from the President. However, it didn't take long for word to spread that is *was* him. Soon, with the call now on speakerphone in my brother's room, every doctor who knew about it was in there listening to the President of the United States trying to cheer up Ed.

"How are you doing?" the President asked him. "Are they treating you well? I'm glad the operation was a success."

My brother thanked him and then asked the President, "Where is my brother?"

"He's right here next to me," the President answered. "When we're finished talking to you, we're going riding."

In all my seventeen years serving the President, I never heard him speak boastfully. His attitude always conveyed his belief that he just *happened* to be president. After his presidency, I was transferred from the ranch detail and was promoted to the ASAIC of the Reagan protective division in Los Angeles. When people praised him or reminded him that he was the one who brought down the Berlin Wall, freeing millions of people, his reply was usually the same: I was just doing my job and what I believed I must do. He didn't like taking credit.

I saw other presidents literally grow old in the White House, but not Reagan. He always stayed even keeled, whether or not things were bad or good. He would not brood when things went wrong, and when they did go wrong, he would call his people in who were more upset than he was and would tell them, "Okay, our plan didn't work. That's my fault. We still need to keep focused on this, and we'll try to do it from a different angle. Let's just all work together." Then he would lift everyone's spirits by telling a joke. His optimism carried not only him but everyone around him.

When things did go right, however, he would not take the credit. He liked giving the credit to other people. He said repeatedly, "Just think what we could accomplish if no one had to take the credit." Just like President Truman, there was a sign on his desk that read: "The buck stops here." In other words, I will take full blame. Yet Reagan would never take full credit.

THE PRESIDENT loved to drive his Jeep around the ranch. When you think about it, he never was able to drive. When he was governor or running for president he didn't drive, and he most certainly didn't drive as president. It was at the ranch that he had the freedom to drive, and that was another reason he loved it. When he'd head out to chop wood, he'd throw the saws into his old, beat-up red Jeep. Dennis and Barney would take the other Jeep, and off they'd go. Together with some of their friends, Mrs. Reagan bought him a blue Jeep as a birthday gift in 1983. Always concerned for his safety, she preferred the newer model.

Still, he loved the old red one. It was a standard shift with a clutch. The four-wheel drive had another shift, not the push buttons they have today. It also had the winch with levers and controls, so you had four sticks in there and a clutch. One day when he was out trimming trees, he kept moving farther and farther away. Finally, I called back to the agents to bring the vehicles up in case we needed them. I wanted the vehicles close to us at all times when we were out on the property. When protecting the president, a second can make all the difference. The other agents called back to me and said, "Roger," but nothing happened. I called them again, which I didn't like to do. Now irritated, I was thinking, *Why am I having to call twice?* Still, I got nothing.

Now I was upset, and the President noticed that I was agitated. I called again. After that, he asked, "What's the matter?" Just when I was about to say I don't know, they called me back. I started laughing and shaking my head. "What are you laughing at?" he asked.

"Well, sir, it just goes to show how we're getting old, and the new agents coming up are very young. I called to get your Jeep up here, because I wanted the Jeep close to you at all times for obvious reasons, but none of these new agents know how to drive a standard shift."

He looked at me and asked, "Well, do you want me to go get it?"

"No, sir. I'll call up one of the guys to be with you, and I'll go get it."

Then he asked, always choosing his words carefully so that he would not insult me, "Well, do you know how to drive a standard shift?" In other words, *don't screw up my Jeep, I don't want to hear that clutch grinding the gears.*

"Yes, sir, I do know how to drive a standard shift," I reassured him.

He laughed and said, "I should have known."

For the President, work was a labor of love. Although he was in great shape, he never was an exercise man. He never did push-ups or lifted weights. Exercise had to have a purpose. For him, that purpose was maintaining the ranch that he loved. His son Ron Reagan once wrote an article for *Esquire* magazine on Father's Day in which he talked about the fact that in our day and age we're used to people working out, exercising. However, he said, his father never went to the gym. Instead, the way his dad worked out was to live a vigorous life. He just worked his ranch and worked the land.

The President just wasn't a push-up type of guy, and he thought jogging was crazy. One of the agents on the detail with me was an avid jogger. At about 165 pounds, Larry was in good shape, and he would wear out his one hundred and twenty dollar running shoes in about a month. He had asked the shift leader if he could run up the hill to the ranch. He would start early so he could make his shift at the scheduled time. The shift leader said, "Fine, run up, take a shower, change, and then take your shift." Larry would run all the way up that seven-mile hill.

He was on post one morning when we were getting the horses ready. I said, "Mr. President, that's the agent I told you about."

I then called to Larry, "Come here. I was telling the President that you're the one who runs up the hill."

The President turned and looked at him and just asked, "Why?" Larry didn't say a word, because he didn't know what to say. When the President uttered that one word, I thought to myself that I knew exactly what he meant by it. *Why would you run up the hill? Don't we have a car for you?*

President Reagan would sometimes forget that he was the leader of the Free World as he tried to deal with the simple problems of ranch life. Occasionally, it would lead to a near crisis. There was a time early on when he had put some goldfish in the pond in front of the house to eat the algae, which was a constant problem. It did not take long, however, for a beautiful blue heron, perched high up on some electrical wires, to discover the fish. (Later these wires were put underground to provide better access for landing helicopters if we needed them.) Naturally the heron began eating the fish. The President took notice and was frustrated by it.

One morning, soon after, I was on post by the tack barn when he came out of his house with his windbreaker on and walked up the path toward me and over to the pond. Before I could tell what he was doing, he raised a pistol and started blasting away at the heron. He wasn't trying to shoot it; he was hoping to scare the bird away for good. When the gunshots echoed through the air, the whole place went crazy.

In an instant, the Secret Service radio was blaring in my ear as everyone tried to figure out where the gunshots were coming from. I tried to calm everyone, but made a poor choice of words. "It's okay," I said calmly in the radio, "Reagan shot."

"Reagan is shot?!" they screamed back. I quickly explained what happened and then looked back over at the President. He was aware of the commotion he had caused.

"I suppose I should have told you I was going to do that, huh?"

I nodded.

After that, the Secret Service held onto all of his firearms for safekeeping.

* * *

THE PRESIDENT was sensible and had simple tastes. For more than forty years, he went to the same barber and the same tailor. He was always impeccably dressed, and he carried himself with poise. He and I could have the same suit on, but I would look like a slob compared to him. He was just one of those people who always looked good. People said that he dyed his hair, but he did not, and he had a naturally rosy color in his cheeks all the time. He brought brown suits back into style. There is a great picture of him by the Rose Garden at the back entrance of the Oval Office leaning against a pillar in a brown suit. Frank Mariani, his tailor, once told me, "John, people usually just don't buy brown suits, but we have orders for brown suits now because of Ronald Reagan." He looked great in brown.

We would go into Mariani's shop in Beverly Hills, a small room on the second floor of an office building. Your typical tailor, Frank was a thin man with a small frame. He was a nice guy who was very conscientious, paying exacting attention to every detail. Frank would always measure the President, but the President's measurements never changed. They were the same in 1944 as they were in 1994. I don't think his weight ever fluctuated more than five pounds, even when he was in the hospital. The President bought conservative suits—not what was in style at the time. He always bought the best white shirts, with just one quarter of an inch of cuff showing. The handkerchief in his suit pocket was always positioned the same way too. His ties were also classics. Not the thin tie or the wide tie or the tie-died color. He always looked impeccable, and while he was careful with his money, his suits were very expensive. He would select suits that he could wear for twenty years and that would always be in style.

Although he always looked great, he wasn't particularly interested in fashion. Mrs. Reagan would call Frank for him and say, "I want him to have a vest. I want him to have this suit." The President liked that, and so did Mrs. Reagan. Her designer was James Galanos. The owner of an old family business, he had a small boutique located in Los Angeles. She would go to him with her requests and spend a lot of time in his office just talking about the designs. Then she would walk back to where all the seamstresses were busy working on their sewing machines making dresses and suits.

She would ask them about a particular detail on a dress, and they would say, "Yes, we can do that. Would you like that ruffle here?"

For many of the White House or other state affairs, Galanos gave Mrs. Reagan gowns to wear. Since she did wear the same dress many times, records were kept. There would be a record of not only the dress and the shoes but also the pocketbook. For example, I wore this on February 10 at such-and-such a speech. The list was kept so she would not wear the same outfit if she went back to the same function the next year. It was a great system. Once I asked her, "Who's going to remember if you wore the same dress?"

"You'd be surprised," she answered.

The President's culinary tastes were simple too. Both he and Mrs. Reagan ate very sensibly. He was in good shape, and Mrs. Reagan would monitor his diet carefully. He wasn't a snacker, and the only time he violated that was when he enjoyed his beloved Jelly Bellies. Still, he did like his desserts after dinner, and when he was served his birthday cake, he would dive right into it.

His favorite meal was macaroni and cheese, and he would eat it off a paper plate with a plastic fork when he was at the ranch. Yet he would be just as much at ease when dining with the Queen of England at Windsor Castle. That has to be some of the most elegant dining in the world. For most people, dining there would be a nerve-racking experience, but not for Ronald Reagan. There was a huge, long table in a gallery-style room with a soaring vaulted ceiling. Seated around that table were some of the most important people in the world, including Margaret Thatcher and her husband Dennis. There was one waiter assigned to each person at the table, and there were at least eight glasses at each setting along with twelve different sizes of forks, three different sizes of knives, and four or five dif- ferent sizes of spoons. The whole process would keep most people on edge.

During our formal dinner with the Queen, I was curiously examining the menu when I noticed the words Firestone Wines from California. The owner of that winery, Brooks Firestone, is a friend of mine, so I took a few extra menus and slid them into the inside pocket of my suit. Coincidentally, I saw Brooks at the airport the next time I flew to California. I said, "You have got to see this." He had no idea the Queen had been selecting his wines. She just happened to like California wine and had chosen Fire- stone. I had thought it was a special account, but it wasn't.

"Can I please have the menu?" Brooks asked me.

"Of course, that's why I brought it."

"John, I want to use this in an advertisement. I'll pay you."

"Brooks, are you kidding? I brought it back for you. You can do whatever you want with it." I suggested he get in touch with the Queen's wine steward and send her a case of his wine.

He did, and he thanked me because he got a response. He talked to them about advertising, and the steward said, "The Queen doesn't endorse anything so if you're looking for that—"

"No, no, no, I'm not looking for that," he reassured them. "John Barletta brought me back a menu."

"Who's John Barletta?"

"He was with the President during his visit to Windsor Castle, and he brought the menu back to show me that the Queen was drinking my wine. I just want people to know that the Queen drinks Firestone wine."

"Well, do it tastefully, but don't mention that the Queen endorsed it," the steward instructed him.

We'd travel to China, and I would realize that I was sitting on a five thousand-year-old chair and eating out of a five thousand-year-old bowl. I'd get a kick out of that. The bowls and plates were gorgeous. In America, a two hundred-year-old rocking chair is considered an antique. No one, however, was allowed to touch the plates, except for the servers. While they claimed it was part of their etiquette, what they were really getting at was don't mess with that plate because you could chip it. Still, even then, the President would be smiling and talking and telling funny stories. He could be regal in elegant situations or completely casual, just knocking the dust off his boots, while eating his macaroni and cheese from a paper plate.

Once we were in Great Britain for an official state visit. We

were both standing in Windsor Castle amidst the fine art, beautiful music, and hundreds of years of history. He whispered, "I'd
still rather be riding."

THE PRESIDENT'S simple, straightforward character didn't
permit him to overlook unfairness, rudeness, or injustice. He was
upset when the news media started stories about how "extrava-
gant" and "insensitive" the First Lady was for buying expensive
china for the White House at the taxpayer's expense during an
economic recession. I was with her when she ordered it. The
United States taxpayers didn't spend one penny for that china,
yet the news media kept printing that they did. I didn't understand that. I was there. She would ask me, "John, am I going
crazy? Weren't you with me?"

"Yes, ma'am. We were in New York. You just selected the
design." Besides, it was time for some new china. They hadn't
had any since the Kennedys. The old collection was broken and
chipped, and a lot of it had been pilfered. When at a formal
White House dinner, many people like to slip one of those cups
or saucers or an ashtray into their pockets as a souvenir. It's very
important to have presentable, elegant china during dinners with
heads of state and other high-ranking military from other countries, but the press was relentlessly unfair about it.

The President was also bothered when he saw other people
behaving rudely. One year at the G-8 Summit, he observed
French president François Mitterand unnecessarily taking Mrs.
Thatcher to task. During a break, he went up to her and said,
"Maggie, I want to apologize for him. That was very rude of him
to talk to you that way, and there was no reason for it."

She just tapped him on the shoulder and said, "That's okay, Ronnie, boys will be boys." In other words, don't you worry about it.

Later, when he and I were alone, I said, "I guess you stuck up for Mrs. Thatcher pretty good."

"Well, he shouldn't have talked to her that way."

"Well," I said, "she didn't seem to mind."

"No, Maggie can handle him, believe me."

Although he rarely talked about the past, he once did tell me a story about an incident that occurred during the years he was traveling for the *General Electric Theater*. On those trips he carried a gun, and one time he intervened to protect a woman. He was in his hotel room on the second floor and had his window open, because it was hot and there was no air-conditioning. Hearing screaming outside his window, he looked out and saw, under the streetlight, a woman who was being accosted. Alarmed and upset, he stuck his head out the window and yelled to the man, "Leave that woman alone!" The guy just looked at him defiantly. So Reagan took his gun out and showed it to that guy, and the young man vanished immediately.

President Reagan's hands were never idle, and when he wasn't doing physical work, he was writing. During his presidency, he wrote thousands of letters, constructed many of his speeches, and was constantly slipping notes to people. I would see him in a meeting—it might be with a foreign leader or with cabinet members—and as one of the cabinet members was discussing a matter, he would write something. Letter writing may have come easily to him because he usually knew just what he wanted to say. His last communication to everyone was through a beautifully written letter. In that letter he told the world, as if speaking from one friend to another, that he had begun the long descent into the place Alzheimer's takes its victims.

The President took simple pleasure in working with his hands, and the ranch was the perfect place for that, whether he was cleaning the horses, cleaning the equipment, or clearing brush. I think he whistled while he worked because he was happy. He wasn't whistling a song, he'd just whistle and say something such as, "Yeah, now, I'll take that. Now, let's do that." He was talking to himself and having a ball. Every once in a while, he'd call Barney and Dennis over and ask them, "What do you think of this?"

He would whistle and hum and he would be working. He always had a plan. When we rode, he would say, "There's a good place to go cut wood this afternoon." I would make a mental note of what marker it was closest to and would then tell Dennis where it was so he could have all the equipment up there ready for the President. I would also tell the shift leader so that he could secure that particular area, and countersniper teams were notified where he would be.

He was always thinking about what he was going to do next. He'd take a limb down, and then he'd say, "Now, if I take that other limb down, maybe we will be able to see through these trees better when we ride by next time. Let's prune this tree up a little bit too."

The next time we'd go riding, he would devise a way to ride by where he had pruned the trees and cut away the brush. He'd say to Mrs. Reagan, "See, honey? We cleared all of this. Now do you see the vistas? You can see right through all these trees and see the beautiful mountains and all the other trees?"

"Yes, dear, I see it. What a wonderful job you guys did." To him, appreciation for his hard work was the best praise he could ever wish for, and knowing that, she would praise him for it all the time.

Sometimes it was difficult to continue on a trail in an area where he wanted to ride. He would say, "Well, tomorrow we'll be able to get through there." After we were finished with our ride, he'd go back to that spot and would start clearing a trail. Dennis would say, "Yes, Mr. President, we can do that." At first they would cut a little bit and then a little bit more and a little bit more. In the end, they would decide to just clear out the whole thing, because that was what he really wanted to do.

Finally, near the end of the day, Dennis would say, "Mr. President, it's time to go."

"Well, maybe—"

"Mr. President, Mrs. Reagan's got dinner."

"Oh, all right."

If Dennis hadn't spoken up, the President would have just kept working. He never wanted to be finished—never. He would have gone at it all night if Mrs. Reagan would have let him.

10

The People He Loved to Be With

As president, Reagan did try to bring the family together and involve them in what he loved to do. We were going to Camp David to go riding one weekend in the early 1980s, and he had invited the whole family—Maureen, Michael, Patti, and Ron, as well as their spouses and children. In the end, Ron, his wife Doria, and Maureen were the only ones who came. The President wanted everything to go just right. On the way up to Camp David, he was talking to me about the weekend. "Now, you know, they don't ride that well." He really wanted them to enjoy their ride together.

"Sir, I've got horses from the Park Rangers. They are very calm and placid animals."

"There will be no trotting," he said. "We'll just take a slow walk with them."

Concerned about his family's safety, he wanted to make sure

that Maureen had a horse that would suit her. I could see that he was struggling with this, so I said, "Mr. President, I have a nice stout horse for Maureen. She'll be fine."

Although the ride went well that day, you could tell that things just seemed forced. He loved his children, but often they seemed so emotionally distant. Ron and Patti could be rebellious, and at times they would cause problems. Early in his father's presidency, Ron was touring with the Joffrey Ballet Company and would travel around the country on a bus. The Secret Service agents were required to travel with him, but he felt uncomfortable under their protection and enjoyed trying to figure out how to avoid them. Ron was young at the time and considered this a harmless game, which from our perspective it was not. It could have literally put the agents in jeopardy as they raced through New York City traffic to find him. To make things run more smoothly, we could have used more cooperation from both Ron and Patti. Ron pretty much kept his distance from the family, rarely visiting his parents.

There was quite a buzz at the White House following Ron's guest appearance on "Saturday Night Live." In one of the skits, he paraded around in his underwear, lip-synching a rock-and-roll song in an imitation of Tom Cruise in the movie *Risky Business*. When I saw the President the next day, he asked me, "Did you see Ron?"

I smiled and said, "He was great, Mr. President," and he smiled too. You could tell he was very proud of his son's performance.

Later in the day, I saw Mrs. Reagan and asked her, "Did he call you and tell you he was going to be on the show?"

"No," she said. I told her I thought he was great, but she was decidedly less enthusiastic than the President was. "John, he was in his *underwear*."

Michael could be testy at times. He too was young, and during a visit to Canada in the mid-1980s, he got into a shouting match with the Royal Canadian Mounted Police (RCMP). Not wanting to leave anyone behind, he wanted to take more friends than the RCMP unmarked vehicle could accommodate. The Mounties rightly opposed this on safety grounds. I was with the Liaison Division of the Secret Service, assigned to be the liaison agent with the foreign embassies. In an effort to smooth things over, I went to the Canadian Embassy in Washington, D.C., and asked our friends from up North, "Can you find a way to fit a few of his friends in the back?"

The decision was made that he could fit as many friends as possible in the backseat while only agents would occupy the front. This compromise prevented a minor disagreement from spinning into a diplomatic incident. Later in life, Michael would mellow. He always admired and loved his father and his father's great legacy. Today he is a successful radio talk show host and is a great supporter of the Navy League, which works to aid the USS *Ronald Reagan* by improving the ship to make it more comfortable for the men and women who serve on it.

At the time, the President's oldest daughter Maureen was probably the closest to her father politically. She was very smart, and, of all the children, she was the most active in his administration. She traveled on several occasions as part of diplomatic missions to countries around the world, and she was a tireless champion of her father. Sometimes this caused political waves, because she was not always easy for the diplomats to deal with. When she visited another country, she could be quick to let the ambassadors know whom they worked for.

The relationship between Maureen and her parents remained solid until the end. After the diagnosis of her father's Alzheimer's, she became a member of the board of directors of the Alzheimer's Association. In 1996, she was diagnosed with malignant melanoma, and by 2001 the tumors had spread to her brain. For five years, she battled skin cancer.

The last time I saw Maureen was in 2000, a year before she died. I had retired from the Secret Service and was visiting the Reagans, because Mrs. Reagan wanted to see the latest puppy that I had named in honor of her husband. As a puppy raiser for Guide Dogs of America, located in Sylmar, California, I train seeing-eye dogs for the blind. Each litter is assigned a letter of the alphabet, and each puppy's name has to start with that letter to keep track of them. This dog, a beautiful black male Lab, was from the R litter. With the school's approval, I named him Rawhide, which was the President's Secret Service code name.

Maureen stopped by while I was there, and we started talking about her melanoma. She told me, "You should have a full body scan from your dermatologist because little things turn into big things." You could see that she was very gentle and loving to both of her parents. A year later to the day, on August 8, 2001, she died. I sent Mrs. Reagan my condolences. Because of his Alzheimer's at that time, the President did not understand that Maureen was gone.

Patti could cause some problems for the First Couple *and* the Secret Service. Sometimes she would leave her house and drive off, without alerting the agents that she was leaving or telling them where she was going. Of course, our fears were that she might be in danger.

Finally, Patti and Ron went to their father and requested that he have the Secret Service protection removed. He agreed but was very direct with them. "The reason they're with you is to protect you and to prevent me from being put into a compromising situation. If something happens and you get kidnapped, or worse, and they try to blackmail me, what can I do? I'm going to have to make the decision on the side of the United States government. You will be on your own. Now do you still really want to disband the details?"

"Yes," they both said.

"All right, as long as I've made myself clear."

As much as she publicly complained about it, Patti knew very well the benefits to having such famous parents. When she wanted something, she would often contact them. There was the time she brought a friend to the White House. She said to her father, "I want you to talk to my friend about the environment, Dad. You're really not hearing the right thing."

I followed them into the Oval Office. Immediately after they sat down, Patti's friend started into a lecture, refusing even to address him as Mr. President. When he tried to respond, she just rudely interrupted him. After a few of her interruptions, he just sat with his hands folded, patiently listening to her. It was supposed to be a ten-minute meeting, but it dragged on for more than twenty minutes. Not wanting to interrupt them, his secretary Kathy Osborne came in to indicate that he had something else scheduled, but he just kept listening to Patti's friend. Finally, he asked in a respectful tone, "Are you done? Can I talk now?"

He then politely went over every issue she had raised. He had allowed the young woman to have all that time because he knew that it was important to Patti.

After President and Mrs. Reagan returned to private life in California, Patti would call her mother and ask for her help when she needed something. One time, I lost my patience with Patti. She had called her mother because she wanted a meeting with a Hollywood CEO. When she arrived at her parents' Bel Air home, she made it known to the agents that she was going to drive her mother to the CEO's home in Malibu. I was on duty in their home that morning. With the Reagans' permission, their garage had been reconstructed by the Secret Service into the command post. One of the agents came and announced the news to me, "Patti wants to drive Mrs. Reagan."

"No, no, she's not driving Mrs. Reagan," I said angrily.

When Mrs. Reagan and Patti came out the front door to leave, I asked Patti, "What are you doing?"

"Well, I thought I would just drive my mother."

I reminded her, "Mrs. Reagan is traveling in a Secret Service vehicle, and you know that. There is special equipment in there."

"Well I guess my reputation preceded me about my driving."

"No, Patti, it's not that."

The doors of the limousine were opened and Patti got in with Mrs. Reagan. I was sitting in the right front seat as we drove off and could clearly hear everything Patti was saying to her mother. She said, "Yeah, Mom, they wouldn't let me drive." Mrs. Reagan wasn't saying anything back to her. So Patti just kept going. "Yeah, I used to outwit those agents. I used to lose them in New York."

Finally I put my arm over the seat, turned my head back,

and, looking directly at her, said, "Patti, do you think it's funny that you play games with the United States Secret Service when their only motive, their only reason to be there, is to protect you—with their lives if necessary?!"

I turned back around and not another word was said. I was just fuming.

When we returned to the Reagans' home, and after Patti had left, I went to see Mrs. Reagan. "I want to apologize for my conversation with your daughter. I was very distraught, and I hope you know where I was coming from. Still, I shouldn't have said that. I should have been more professional."

PRESIDENT AND MRS. REAGAN had several close friends. They had known these people for decades. When you are in politics, it is always difficult to figure out who is a real friend and who just wants something from you. The Reagans solved that problem by staying closest to the people they had known in Hollywood before their political life, as well as a few good friends from their years in California politics. With all their success, they were mindful never to desert their dearest friends. Even when they moved into the White House, it seems that their relationships never changed.

As I mentioned earlier, one of the President's closest friends was Judge Bill Clark. The Clarks are an old California family with a rich heritage in the Central Valley. They have been ranchers for generations, and they love horses deeply. It was Bill who gave Mrs. Reagan the horse, No Strings, as a gift.

Their friendship flourished even more when they were out riding together. One of the places they rode was the FBI Academy and Marine Training Center in Quantico, Virginia. I clearly remember the horse that was selected for the President that day—a diminutive mare. It just didn't fit the status of the president of the United States. Still, he enjoyed the ride with his friend Bill, and after the ride, he thanked the supervisor of the stables. He was always gracious. I made sure, however, that from then on he had a horse that was suited for a president who knew how to ride.

In the early days of his administration, Austria gave the President one of their prized Lipizzan stallions. Lipizzans are short-coupled horses, stocky with big necks, long flowing manes, and long tails that touch the ground. When they are babies, they are black, but as they mature, they turn into a gray, which really looks white. Though appreciative of the kind gift, the President knew that this stallion was not the type of horse that he would choose to ride. Lipizzans are beautiful show horses. General Patton saved this line of horses during the Second World War. When the Germans marched into Austria, they were going to kill them, but the General was a horse lover and found a way to save them.

President Reagan faced a dilemma. He not only didn't have a place in Washington, D.C. to keep the Lipizzan, but the stallion would not fare well at the ranch either. Bill was the one who volunteered to help the President. He took the horse under his care, and for a short time kept him at the U.S. Park Police training barn. Bill rode that horse almost every morning when he was in Washington, and I would accompany him on those rides whenever I was able to. Later, the Lipizzan was shipped to Bill's ranch in Paso Robles, California.

Keeping the same circle of friends, the President and Mrs. Reagan did just about everything with them. The First Couple visited regularly with Alfred and Betsy Bloomingdale, founders of the famed department store. Betsy had a sense of style and grace that Mrs. Reagan thoroughly enjoyed. A tall, thin woman, Betsy knew her clothes. She would take Mrs. Reagan through one of the stores in Beverly Hills and point out the stitching and quality of the items. The clothes in these stores did not have price tags on them, so Mrs. Reagan would ask, "What does this cost?" When Betsy told her the price, Mrs. Reagan would just say, "Oh, my."

Charlie Wick and his wife, Mary, were also good friends. Charlie had been in the entertainment business, and he and Mary got along famously with the Reagans.

Marj Everett would also become a part of the Reagans' inner circle of friends. At the time she owned Hollywood Park, one of the most beautiful horse racing tracks in the country. Every time she visited the White House, she would bring cookies that she had baked in her oven in California for the First Couple as well as the Secret Service. When the Reagans went to her house, she would have more cookies waiting. On one occasion, she held a party at her home and all the top jockeys were there—Eddie Arcaro, Willie Shoemaker, and Chris McCarron. President Reagan was a great fan of horse racing and enjoyed talking with the jockeys.

Mrs. Everett was very friendly and could be insistent. "You are going to sit with us at the dining table," she told the Secret Service agents at that party.

"No, no, Mrs. Everett, we don't do that," I told her. "That's impossible."

"All right. Then you will eat in the kitchen."

"Ma'am, we are on duty. We don't want to eat."

"*You will eat.*"

After issuing her command, she headed off into the crowd to tell Mrs. Reagan.

"Nancy, Nancy, they won't eat. Come say something."

Needless to say, moments later we *were* in the kitchen, and we *were* eating.

Another important guest at every party was Merv Griffin. He'd play the piano and sing until Johnny Mathis showed up. Then Johnny would sing while Merv played for him.

Frank Sinatra was another dear friend. Although he was a world-famous celebrity, up close he was just a wonderful person. President Ford was also a friend of Frank's. The agents told me that when they would go to his mansion in Palm Springs during Ford's administration, Frank and his mother would both be in the kitchen making pasta sauce and cooking spaghetti. Frank always insisted the agents would eat something. If they were still on duty, he made sure that they knew there would be plenty left for them when they could eat.

The First Couple and he would have a grand time together. Frank and Mrs. Reagan would dance, and there would be plenty of singing and laughing. Because they were so close, rumors about their relationship floated around. (Many remember the song, "Nancy with the Laughing Face," Sinatra had performed for her at the inauguration.) President Reagan would laugh about it. "You were in the paper again with Frank," he would tell Nancy and then look over at me.

I'd say, "Sir, I know nothing. Right, Mrs. Reagan? That's what you told me to say?" He would laugh, and she would have that little glint in her eye.

Many of the Reagans' best friends were extremely affluent. They were captains of industry or major players in Hollywood, and while people often assume that the Reagans were wealthy like many of their friends, they really were not. One of the reasons Mrs. Reagan eventually sold the ranch to Young America's Foundation was that she needed the money. Hiring caregivers to help her when the President was diagnosed with Alzheimer's was not cheap. In fact, when they moved out of the White House, some of their friends got together and bought a house for them in Bel Air. The President insisted that they would pay them back, and they did.

After the Reagans left Washington, they were often asked, "Do you miss being in the White House? Do you miss Washington, D.C.?"

Both the President and Mrs. Reagan would always answer saying, "No, but we really do miss the people and the friends we made there."

In the world of politics, the national leader the President was the closest to was Mrs. Thatcher. The British prime minister was the "Iron Lady," tough and uncompromising. When she and the President discussed something, they were always straightforward and direct in their conversations. "Maggie, this is how it's going to have to be."

"Ronnie, this is the bottom line."

When they needed something, they simply asked each other for it and expected the other to deliver it. "Ronnie, I need something."

"What do you need, Maggie?"

Their relationship was not formal, and Mrs. Thatcher was

the only person other than Mrs. Reagan who could get away with calling him Ronnie. President Reagan always admired her, and his friendship with her was important to him both in the political sphere and personally.

ONE OF REAGAN'S little known but great escapes from the stresses of life was his membership in the men's riding group called Rancheros Visitadores. Started in 1930, the initial idea was that ranchers would ride around from ranch to ranch in the Santa Barbara area to help each other. If they needed to gather some cattle or if they wanted to do some branding, they did it together as friends. It began with four men. Today the membership includes men from every walk of life, and no matter what the rider's profession, he is an important part of the group. For some families, Rancheros has become a legacy. In the Clark family, Bill's father and grandfather were members early on. Bill is also now a member as well as his two sons, Pete and younger brother Paul.

Every year on the first Friday of May, the Rancheros gather for a week of riding and fellowship. During that week, the group comes together to share their love of horses. You don't talk business or make deals, and no one puts on airs, no matter who they are. These riders are friends for life.

The days are spent on a ride, which is an impressive sight as hundreds of men move across the beautiful ranch lands of central California. At night there is eating, drinking, and live music, and at one time, everyone from the Sons of the Pioneers to Roy Rogers took the stage and sang old cowboy songs. The unity and camaraderie you experience lasts all your life. If you need something, anytime, you call up a fellow Ranchero. When you call and announce to the secretary "I'm a Ranchero," that is all it takes. Although the fellow Ranchero may be the CEO of a major corporation, the next voice you usually hear is his. The doors are opened for you at once.

President Reagan loved the Rancheros and considered his membership one of the great joys of life. He joined in 1969. Later, he became an honorary Ranchero, a title reserved for very few members. Since it's an all-male club, naturally, Mrs. Reagan couldn't go, and frankly she didn't want to. It was for "the boys," she would say.

All the first-year guests camp together out in the woods, some sleeping on the ground with their saddles, just as you might see in the cowboy movies. The undersides of most saddles are fleece lined, and some of the fellows just turn their saddles over and put their heads on them.

President Reagan didn't make it to Rancheros during his years in Washington. He was too concerned that the presence of the Secret Service, his military aide, his doctor, and the WHCA and staff who traveled with him everywhere, would be too disruptive. Instead, he would call and talk to the group over a loud speaker, with everyone gathered around listening to him. "How are you guys doing?" he asked when I was a first-year guest. "I wish I was out there with you. How's John Barletta doing?" I was embarrassed.

Trev Povah, who was a friend of the President's, was a big kidder. "He's doing all right, Mr. President, but he's fallen off his horse twice so far." Everyone went "Oh, oh," and then laughed.

The President, never at a loss for words, responded, "Well, Trev, you must have given him a bad horse." I was so proud that the President had stuck up for me.

Whenever I returned to the White House from my vacation time with the Rancheros, the President was always very interested to hear how the week went.

Each year, we go down below from our camps to the *enramada*, amidst the grand oak trees, to pay our respects to those Rancheros we lost during the previous year. *Enramada* is a place of worship to honor the end of a person's life. The Franciscan Fathers were the ones to introduce this to the Indians in the 1700s. A very special place for the Rancheros, there is a statue of a cowboy with his head bowed, holding his hat in his hand. Near the statue is a huge piece of wood, on which small metal plaques, all equal in size, are placed. Each plaque bears a Ranchero's name and his date of death. On the massive piece of wood, there are more than one thousand names at this time honoring those who have died since 1930.

There is a ceremony during which Bill Clark, who is the chair, gives the eulogy. With soft guitar music playing in the background, someone reads a poem about the death of the cowboy. Next a church bell is rung, and the best friend or possibly the son of the departed member brings the deceased's cowboy hat to the altar on which there is a plain, wooden cross. This goes on with the bell being rung each time a hat is brought forward, until there is one on the altar for each Ranchero who has died during the year. Throughout the ceremony, the rest of the Rancheros are still atop their horses in their saddles with their hats off and their heads bowed, reflecting on the lives of those who came before. After the last hat has been left at the altar, everyone puts their cowboy hats back on, and as a group, we slowly ride away in a vast expanse of silence except for the noise of hooves and neighing. Most of the tough cowboys have at least a few tears in their eyes.

After he left the White House, President Reagan made two more trips to Rancheros. For one of those, he had been nominated as Grand Marshal of the parade that marks the beginning of the rodeo. The American flag is carried in front, followed by the California flag. The President rode in Bill Clark's wagon, wearing one of those old wool jackets and his cowboy hat. At the conclusion of the parade, we always put on our own rodeo. The year President Reagan served as Grand Marshal, he returned to the camping area after the rodeo. There, he was surrounded by hundreds of Rancheros who had gathered to see and hear him. He was just telling stories in the midst of plenty of laughter, but he was starting to slow down. Not able to stay very long, he and I had worked out a signal in advance that meant it was time to go. I played the role of the enforcer saying, "Mr. President, I'm sorry but we have to leave now." Of course everyone booed *me*.

"Mr. President, is there just one more story?" someone asked.

He looked to me for the answer. "Well, are you sure we have to go, John?"

"Mr. President, you know the deal. We have to leave now."

He shrugged his shoulders and said, "Well, okay." It was his way of being able to get home and rest without disappointing the fellows. Of course he did tell one last story.

During my seventeen years of serving him and twenty-four years of knowing him, the amazing thing I learned about him was that whether or not he was meeting with Gorbachev at a summit meeting or sitting in the saddle with his friends at Rancheros, he was always the same person. He never put on airs. He was genuine.

While the President clearly loved his family and his friends, he could also be distant from people, and that emotional distance was extended to some degree to everyone in his life except for Nancy. He loved to be with people, but he also loved his solitude. When he had free time, the ranch is where he wanted to go, not a swank Hollywood party. He liked to be outdoors, riding a horse for hours with no one else around. I also think that during both his childhood and early years of adulthood he was bruised by some painful experiences. He loved his parents, but he was on his own much of the time. His father was both a dreamer and a drunk. That left his mother Nelle in charge of the Reagan home. Since he never had much of a relationship with his father, it was probably difficult for him to know exactly how to interact with his own children. He certainly tried, but those relationships were at times difficult and awkward.

Always warm and gracious to his friends, he had known many of them for fifty years, but in the end, I'm not sure if he ever completely opened up to them and if they really understood him. There was a part of him that was always private.

11

The Gipper's Smile

One of the things I noticed while working in the Secret Service is that presidents literally get old while living in the White House—except for Reagan. There were times when he actually seemed to get younger, even though he was already in his seventies. I'm convinced this was because he was an optimist at heart. When things did go wrong, he never forgot the power of having a sense of humor.

He would use humor in situations some people would find surprising. There were times during an intense discussion among the cabinet that he would suddenly start telling a story. Some people wondered: *Is he really paying attention?* He was listening, but from what he was hearing, people had lost perspective. So to diffuse the tension and get the discussion back into calmer waters, he would engage everyone with a funny story or a joke.

The President had great stories that he loved to tell, yarns that he had collected over the years. He could also be spontaneously funny. Never taking himself too seriously, he would use self-deprecating humor. He also used humor to reveal a deeper truth or to make someone feel better.

One morning at the ranch, the President asked me if there was someone new on detail that day. New agents usually didn't go to the ranch, but this morning it was a little different. "Well, sir, matter of fact, there is, and he's one of the riders. He'll be going out with us today."

The horses were all saddled, and President Reagan said, "Well, why don't you have him come down? I'd like to say hello."

I called on the radio to the new agent. "*Rawhide* would like you to come down. He wants to talk to you."

Most of the agents who worked at the ranch never really got a chance to speak with the President, so for him, this was a big moment. Excited, the young agent decided to put on a bit of a show. He was on his horse close to the top of a nearby hill. Standing in the stirrups, he came down the hill at a high trot. You should never do that, but the young agent was in a hurry to see the President. As he came around the corner near the barn, there was a small ditch from the water runoff. When he hit that ditch, the horse stumbled, and the agent somersaulted right over the horse's head. Amazingly, he landed on his feet with the reins still in his hands. The President just looked at me and asked, "Say, John, does he always dismount that way?"

President Reagan liked to tell self-effacing stories that were quite funny. He knew that his critics thought he was too old and not very sharp. To disarm them, he would come up with the funniest stories that *seemed* to confirm their point but actually showed how comfortable he was with himself.

He once recounted a visit he made to Mexico when he was governor of California. Representing the United States at a function across the border, he delivered a speech to a large crowd there. When he was finished speaking, he heard only scattered applause as he sat down. He felt embarrassed that the speech had been received unenthusiastically. When the next speaker, who spoke in Spanish, got tremendous applause from the audience for his talk, he became even more embarrassed. To hide his discomfort, he decided to clap louder and longer than anyone else did. After a few minutes of this, the American ambassador to Mexico leaned over to him and said, "I wouldn't do that if I were you. He's interpreting your speech."

President Reagan had precious few enemies because he was such a likeable person. Tip O'Neill, the Speaker of the House and a tough liberal, fought the President's agenda at every step. Through it all, though, the two men would swap stories and remain on friendly terms. President Reagan seemed to have the same kind of relationship with the news media. While most of them considered him a simpleton, he never allowed their assumptions to define him. He truly enjoyed poking fun at them and was usually friendly, even when reporters like Sam Donaldson could become nasty with him.

The news media were always on the hunt, trying to cover his every move when he was at the ranch. The Reagans might have wanted privacy, but the news media came up with ingenious ways to chip away at it. Because the ranch was located up on a hillside, it was impossible for them to see anything from the perimeter or the front gate. Not to be deterred, some intrepid journalists found a spot on a nearby hillside to camp out on. Using a massive telephoto lens mounted on the back of a truck, they could get a good picture of the President riding, even though he was one thousand yards away. The Secret Service, of course, was well aware of this, and we informed the President about the intrusion. Soon he knew where along the trails the photojournalists could see him. One morning we were out riding, and the President asked, "John, are they up there again today? Are they watching us?"

"Yes, sir, I believe they are."

Then he got one of those mischievous grins of his. "Can they see us right now?"

"Yes they can."

"Well, why don't I grab my chest and fall off the horse, pretending that I've had a heart attack?"

I turned quickly to look at Mrs. Reagan, who just rolled her eyes.

"Mr. President," I said with some urgency, "please don't do that." Images of the stock market plunging, the Soviet Union maneuvering its forces, and Washington, D.C., falling into a panic flashed before me. He was disappointed, I think, that his little prank couldn't be carried out.

On one of his post–White House trips, the President was talking with some of the Secret Service agents during a flight to Japan. We were chatting on the plane when he said to Special Agent in Charge (SAIC) Garrick Newman, "If you ever need another weapon, I've got one here." He then showed us a snub-nosed revolver that was tucked away in his briefcase. When traveling overseas, guns are always a touchy subject, even for Secret Service agents.

Oh my God, I thought, *where did he get that?*

The President told us that he had traveled with a pistol

before. "Now, fellows," he said, "they don't search me, you know."

"No, they don't search you, Mr. President."

Garrick took control of the weapon and thanked the President. Reagan was always full of surprises.

For President Reagan, the news media were a constant source of bemusement. Sam Donaldson, an aggressive reporter who was with ABC News in the 1980s, was always trying to get to the President. After the Iran-Contra scandal broke, in which the United States was found to be shipping weapons illegally to Iran and diverting the profits to the Contras, the President still didn't lose his sense of humor. "I have to admit we considered making one final shipment to Iran," he told some friends, "but no one could figure out how to get Sam Donaldson in a crate."

Some reporters were angry because they wanted the President to hold more press conferences. Once a reporter shouted to him at the White House, "You wouldn't turn down our invitation to come talk to us, would you, Mr. President?"

The President grinned and said, "If I can choose the subjects, no."

Another time a reporter was pressing the President over the lack of news media access during the invasion of Grenada. Would he consider allowing the press to travel with the American soldiers next time? President Reagan responded by saying that he probably would let the news media go—in the front row of the landing craft "so they'll be the first off."

In a subtle way I think the President, through his humor, helped the news media not to take themselves too seriously either. On his seventy-second birthday, Mrs. Reagan brought a cake to a press conference and gave a piece to each of the reporters. As they gobbled down the treat, one of them cracked to the President, "You understand, we won't sell out for a piece of cake. No deals." The President just smiled and in an instant responded, "Oh, you've sold out for less than that."

Whenever a president goes anywhere, he is constantly getting questions fired at him. Sometimes the questions are tough. Other times, they are just inane.

A reporter asked him, "What are you going to tell the Chinese ambassador?"

"Hello," he said with the tilt of his head.

During the 1984 presidential campaign, a reporter asked him, "What about Mondale's charges?"

"He ought to pay for them."

Reporters would take jabs at him. Yet most of the time he rose above them, coming up with something even more humorous. At the White House correspondent's dinner one year, a journalist went to the podium and said, "I've seen it reported that you're just a president of image and no substance, but I understand that you often take home serious reports and documents to read at night. I'm also told that you often pick up one of those serious reports or documents to study—during the commercials."

President Reagan stood up, went to the mike, and responded, "You made a slight mistake. I read the papers while the news is on. I watch the commercials."

During the horror of the assassination attempt his humor was on great display. Many people may recall that as he entered the hospital, he looked at the doctors and said, "Gee, I hope you are all Republicans." He kept this up over the next several days as the medical staff desperately worked to save his life and a nervous nation waited for updates. He quipped to the nurses, "Gee, if I had this much attention in Hollywood, I'd have stayed there."

While he was recovering in his hospital bed, his political advisor Lyn Nofziger came by and reported that everything in Washington was "running normally." President Reagan looked up and asked, "What makes you think I'd be happy about that?"

Agent Tim McCarthy told me a story years later about how the President called him to his hospital room to visit. During their conversation the President said, "Say, Tim, what's wrong with this Hinckley kid? Delehanty, Brady, McCarthy, Reagan—what's he got against Irishmen?"

Oftentimes, the President's humor was about more than laughs. Those people who believed that his jokes were just horse-play missed the deeper meaning of what he said when he was being funny. A gifted joke teller, he could sometimes express more with just one humorous line than someone else could in a thirty-minute lecture. He once shared with me the details of an experience that he had when he was governor in the 1960s. A group of student body presidents from the nine California university campuses and some of their other student officers asked to have a meeting with him. Anxious to establish some sort of dialogue with the students, then Governor Reagan immediately said yes. The students all arrived at the meeting dressed in T-shirts and jeans, and some were even barefoot. Their spokesperson opened the meeting. "Governor," he said, "it's impossible for you to understand us, to understand our generation."

Trying to move the conversation along, Reagan responded, "Well, I know more about being young than you do about being old."

The young man persisted. "No, I'm serious. You can't understand your own sons and daughters. You didn't grow up in a world of instant electronic communications, of cybernetics, of men computing in seconds what it once took months or even years to do, of jet travel, nuclear power, and journeys into space and the moon."

When he was finally finished, Reagan said, "You are absolutely right. My generation didn't have those things when we were growing up. We invented them."

The President loved to tell jokes about how absurd the Soviet system was. Two guys were standing in a line at a vodka store shortly after Gorbachev had placed restrictions on the sale of vodka. They were there for half an hour, then an hour, then an hour and a half.

"I'm sick of this," one of the guys finally said. "I'm going over to the Kremlin to shoot Gorbachev."

The man left but returned about an hour later.

"Well, did you shoot him?" the other man asked.

"Hell, no," he responded. "The line up there is even longer than this one."

President Reagan also liked to share humorous stories about those who held the office before him. One true story he told was about a time Lyndon Johnson was leaving the South Lawn of the White House. There were two helicopters waiting, and he happened to go toward the wrong one. One of the security guards stepped up to him. He really didn't want to since the press was there, but decided that he should. "Mr. President," he said, "that's your helicopter over there."

Lyndon stopped and said, "Son, they're all mine."

There were times when the President's humor would get

him in trouble. Every Saturday morning, he would prepare for his weekly radio broadcasts. There were usually plenty of guests there to watch. For them, it was an opportunity to shake the President's hand and to chat with him. On one of these mornings when it came time to test the microphone and his voice level, the President leaned forward and said, "Ladies and Gentlemen, I have outlawed Russia. We begin bombing in five minutes." Of course he was kidding around and everyone chuckled, finding it funny, but the crew of the WHCA had the microphone on live, and everyone in the world heard what he said. Seizing it as an opportunity to show that the President really was reckless, some of his critics tried to make a mini-scandal out of it.

There were those who felt the entire WHCA crew should have been fired. The President, however, wouldn't hear of it. He refused to let anyone fire the crew.

The President could be very forgiving, and sometimes he did it with humor. There was an incident I was involved in one morning at the ranch. To keep the mouse population in check, there were cats running wild at the ranch. Before the President came up for his ride that morning, one of those cats was walking along a fence post of the corral when suddenly, for whatever reason, it jumped on the head of an agent's horse. The horse, trying to get rid of the cat, reared up and flipped his head up, sending the cat into the air. When the cat hit the ground, the horse literally pummeled him to death with his front hooves. At that point, my supervisor came running out. "What happened?" he asked.

I explained everything to him, but he was upset. "You are going to have to tell the President that one of our horses killed his cat."

Now the President didn't even interact with these cats, because they weren't pets. They were just ranch cats.

"Well, sir, maybe you could tell him that."

My supervisor just shook his head. "No, no, you tell him while you are out riding."

After the ride, my boss asked me, "Did you tell him?"

I shook my head and said, "No, I did not."

"John, I told you to tell him."

"Well, sir, there's a problem. It turns out that that's his favorite cat. In fact, at Thanksgiving, he brings that cat in to have turkey with him. Hopefully, he'll think that he just ran away or maybe that he is missing because he was eaten by a coyote."

The next day when I saw the President, I said, "Sir, one of the cats jumped on the head of an agent's horse, and while trying to get rid of the cat, the horse accidentally killed it."

The President stood there for a moment thinking and then said, "I don't think it was an accident. I think he meant to kill that cat."

Humor was a way for Ronald Reagan to deal with the realities and burdens of the office he held. That was certainly one of the reasons that he told humorous stories, but most of the time he told them not for his own benefit, but for others. With a funny story, he could lift people's spirits and remind them not to take themselves or their predicaments too seriously. For President Reagan, humor was often a selfless act.

12

Closing Scene

The early years after President Reagan left the White House were wonderful times. He traveled around the globe to give speeches and to meet world leaders. Still the ranch was never far from his thoughts, and it was atop his horse that he probably spent more time than he did anywhere else. Even though a horse had thrown him during his trip to Mexico, it didn't lessen his love of riding. Just as he did with everything in life, he climbed right back on.

January 20, 1989, was the President's last day in the White House, and he went to the Oval Office for just one more look. So much had happened there. He was not really leaving with sadness, but instead with a sense of accomplishment. When I had watched other presidents get ready to go, I sensed that they were going to miss the power and the pomp and circumstance. However, as President Reagan prepared to leave, he seemed completely at peace with the whole thing. While flying over Washington, D.C., later that day on *Marine One*, he said, "For eight years I've tried my best. All in all, not bad. Not bad at all."

He wished he could have done more, but he said that during the first four years, he had to spend all his time on the economy and the military to get the country back on its feet. He wanted to do other things, but those were the two most important at the time.

The President closed the door to the Oval Office, and then he went with Mrs. Reagan to the State Dining Room where they said their last goodbye to the White House domestic staff. President Reagan was popular with the staff members. He had a habit of always asking them "How are you today?" even if they were dusting the furniture. After all the tearful goodbyes, it was finally time to go.

President and Mrs. Reagan accompanied the Bushes to the inauguration to witness the swearing-in ceremony. George H. W. Bush was now the forty-first president of the United States, and the Reagans boarded *Marine One* for the short trip to Andrews Air Force Base. As they circled over the nation's capital one final time, President Reagan told his wife, "Look dear, there's our bungalow." When they arrived at Andrews, they boarded *Air Force One* for the flight home.

There was a large crowd waiting for them when the plane touched down in California. Hundreds of friends welcomed them home, and the University of Southern California marching band played some wonderful tunes. They enjoyed a brief party and then headed to their new home.

Mrs. Reagan had found a comfortable one-story, ranch-style house in Bel Air, an upscale community that sits next to Beverly Hills. The home has a swimming pool, and a tall, brick wall surrounds part of the property. (Their street number was 666, but President Reagan asked the number to be changed to 668, because according to the Bible, 666 is the "Mark of the Beast.")

After their friends had left, their emotions finally came pouring out. They held each other and tears welled from their eyes. Their eight years in the White House were over.

The former President set up an office in a beautiful high rise in Los Angeles' Century City. There, he would greet visitors and guests. The office was decorated with pictures of his family and of world leaders he admired, including Dwight Eisenhower and Margaret Thatcher. There were also paintings of horses and some of the beautiful Annenberg Paul Rossi statues. One adorned his desk. It was a stunning piece of art that depicted a man on horseback.

In those early post-Presidential years, the former President's schedule was hectic. In 1989, he visited London, Paris, New York, and Washington, and in 1990, he went to San Francisco, Seattle, Berlin, Warsaw, Leningrad, Moscow, Rome, New York, Dixon, Illinois, and Cambridge, England. Yet there was one place all those travels could not keep him from—his beloved ranch. Every month from January through July and September through November, he managed to squeeze in a ranch visit. He kept an equally busy schedule in 1991, but still managed to fit in a monthly visit.

I HAD NOW KNOWN the President for more than a decade. During that entire time, his memory had been incredible. He could remember the names of friends that he had not seen in forty years, and he could tell stories down to the smallest detail, which I sometimes would later confirm as being completely accurate.

In late 1993, President Reagan flew to Chicago to deliver a speech. Mrs. Reagan was with him, and once they got to their hotel, he seemed confused. Turning to Mrs. Reagan, he said, "I'm afraid I don't know where I am."

In early 1994, I sensed that his memory was faltering. He would try to remember a name, and when you looked at his eyes, you could tell that he was searching. I learned about his Alzheimer's about a week before the public did. It was not a complete surprise to me, since I had noticed changes, not only in his memory, but also in his horse-riding abilities. He was forgetting things more often, and when we went out riding, he would make mistakes—the sort of mistakes that not even a rookie rider would make.

Mrs. Reagan brought the staff together and shared with us about what was to come. The President had received word back from the Mayo Clinic concerning his brain scan. He had Alzheimer's. I was amazed at how courageous and gracious Mrs. Reagan was in both confronting her husband's disease and dealing with all the challenges.

For the President, it was a particularly troubling diagnosis. Not so much for what he feared it might do to him, but instead for what it would mean for the people around him. His mother Nelle had been afflicted with the disease, as had his younger brother Neil. He had watched both of them descend into a world in which they did not recognize those who loved them, and they could no longer care for themselves. I think he was most concerned about what this would mean to Nancy. He often said that his life began when he met Nancy. They had cared for each other deeply, and now she would also be his caregiver. As the nation had done following the assassination attempt more than a decade earlier, it would again admire her strength and love for her husband. This time, however, the ordeal would be long, and there would be no recovery.

In his final letter to the country he loved, the President wrote, "Unfortunately, as Alzheimer's disease progresses, the family often bears a heavy burden. I only wish there was some way I could spare Nancy from this painful experience."

When it all started, he would ask for me. One of the aides would say, "The President wants to see you." I'd go to him and he'd be staring at something. "John, I know I'm supposed to do something with this, but I can't think of it. Would you help me?" He was having difficulty remembering how to buckle the cinch, which is what goes around the horse's girth that holds the saddle in place. Sure enough, he had it on wrong. From the time that started happening, I would have my horse already saddled when he came up, so I could watch him tack up his horse. Often, he would put something in his hand and then hesitate. That would tell me he was having trouble. I would just take his hand and move it to the right position. A big smile would come over his face, "That's what I was trying to do." Those tough times drew us even closer.

As the disease continued its course, he relied on me even more. We were just about back from our ride one day when El Alamein threw a fit. There were ways to get in front of the President to try to help out, but that just made El Alamein act worse. I had to get off my horse and grab the President's rein and walk El Alamein, otherwise he was going to dump the President. I could tell El Alamein was getting ready to explode. He was pitching his head, dancing sideways, and crow hopping.

Earlier, the President would have been able to control

El Alamein, and probably the worst thing you can do to someone who knows how to ride is to step in as I did. The President, however, didn't say a word. We both knew he needed my help. When it was over, he said, "Thank you, John. I don't know what got into him."

Our bond became so strong that there were times it surprised not only me but Mrs. Reagan too. In those last years, she would say to me, "You know, you two hardly even talk to each other anymore," but so often we communicated without actually speaking. He knew the meaning of my actions, and I knew the meaning of his. The strength of our relationship was evident one time soon after his diagnosis. One morning, he was all dressed for his ride when Mrs. Reagan called me at the command post, "John, will you come down here, Ronnie's having a problem."

My immediate thought was, *Is he hurt?* There was already an agent down there, but I was always prepared to fly out the door, so I rushed to the house and asked, "What's the matter?"

"Will you tell my husband that you're ready to go riding? He won't leave." Mrs. Reagan had a technique she used if she wanted the President to get going. She would use the line: "You need to go, because people are waiting." He would never ever want to keep people waiting. It was so impolite.

"Who's he waiting for?" I asked.

"The electrician."

"Did something break?"

"No, John."

"Mr. President," I asked, "is something broken that you need an electrician for?"

"No," he answered.

She looked at me again and said, "See? Honey, you're keeping the boys waiting." She wanted him to go riding and just let this pass.

It was then I said, "Do you mean the *General Electric Theater* you were the host of?"

He turned to Mrs. Reagan and exclaimed, "Yes, I was reminiscing about G. E.! That's it! He knows! That's it!"

He just stood there smiling, because someone knew what he was trying to say. "Mrs. Reagan," I said, "I'm getting about one step behind him as far as bad memory is concerned." I just knew what he was trying to say, what he was thinking about.

She laughed, shook her head, and asked, "And now we can go riding?"

"Yes," I answered. "Now we can go riding."

However, things continued to deteriorate. I went to Mrs. Reagan and said, "Mrs. Reagan, he's making too many mistakes up there. I can't protect him from himself. He's making rookie mistakes, and he's been riding fifty-five years. A new rider wouldn't make these mistakes. I don't think he should ride anymore. It's getting that dangerous."

"Then you have to tell him, John."

"I don't want to tell him that, Mrs. Reagan. You need to tell him that."

"No," she said with tears in her eyes. "I can't." Mrs. Reagan had the wisdom always to know just what was right for the President. "John, you've got to talk to him and tell him, because he'll understand, and he'll take it better if you tell him."

I did not want to do that, but soon after lunch that day, she called for me at the command post. "Now would be the time, John."

"Mrs. Reagan, I don't want to do this."

"John, we've talked about it."

Tentatively, I walked down to the house, knocked on the door, and went inside. He was sitting by the fireplace, reading. He was an avid reader. He'd go to sleep with a book on his chest just about every night. "Mr. President," I said, "we had a lot of trouble out there this morning, didn't we?"

"Yeah, I did." Even in the bad times, he was still polite. I wanted to make it seem like I had been the problem—but that was just not the case.

I went on, "It's just at the point where this riding isn't working out. Sir, I don't think you should ride anymore." Knowing him like I did and understanding what horseback riding meant to him, I felt like I was telling someone I don't think he should breathe anymore. I was now practically in tears.

He got up and put his hands on my shoulders and said, "It's okay, John. I know." That was it. We never rode again. We never talked about it. He could see how upset I was, and he was trying to make *me* feel okay. That was the kind of guy he was. Later on, he gave me his Dehner three-buckle brown field boots, his saddle, and his Ranchero's horseshoe, a symbol given to all members, to remember him by. From one rider to another, you couldn't ask for more intimate gifts.

Although the President tried to keep an active schedule, his memory loss was increasing. The home that they had expected to use for entertaining friends was slowly converted into a place where Mrs. Reagan would care for her husband. Throughout those difficult years, she remained gentle with him. She would hold his hand and kiss him on the cheek or forehead, and he would sit for hours, just patting her hand while she talked to him. Oftentimes, he would smile when she spoke, and there was a sparkle in his eyes.

Mrs. Reagan constantly worried about the President's health. He was less active now, and she was conscious of his weight. Other than our walks in the park, he rarely did much other physical activity. Of course he still loved Jelly Bellies. Herm Rowland, the owner of the company in Northern California that makes Jelly Bellies, always made sure that he had an ample supply for President Reagan. When Reagan came into his office in Los Angeles, he would sneak a handful into his coat pocket when Mrs. Reagan wasn't looking. Eventually, she discovered them and called the staff together.

"What are these Jelly Bellies doing in his pocket?" she asked.

The word went out—no Jelly Bellies for the President. Everyone was put on alert. Even with these restrictions, the former leader of the Free World would find a way to sneak a few. Once, when I was riding with him in the elevator, I noticed a small bulge in his coat pocket.

"All right, Mr. President, give them to me."

"What?"

"You know what. Now you know Mrs. Reagan is going to get mad at me if you come home with a pocket full of Jelly Bellies." He emptied his pocket and gave them to me.

Then I said, "Mr President, I need all of them."

He made a face and reached into his other suit-coat pocket and gave me the rest of them, saying. "How about we just eat the black ones?"

I said, "Okay," and we did.

In late summer 1995, we made a trip to the ranch. It was a painful one for Mrs. Reagan. We drove up as we always did.

However, unlike every other visit, the President did not seem to be filled with much anticipation. Usually, he would time the trip and watch eagerly as we made the winding drive up to the mountainside entrance. This time, he slept in the back seat.

When we finally reached the property, he woke up, but instead of talking about this ranch, he started talking about the one he owned decades ago in Malibu. He had them confused in his mind. Mrs. Reagan started crying. The Alzheimer's had progressed so far that he couldn't even recognize his beloved Rancho del Cielo. He looked around and said, "I thought we sold this place."

Mrs. Reagan just looked at me. I could feel her heart sink. We were supposed to stay for several days, but she said, "John, we're going home tomorrow. I came here just to see about this, just to see his beloved ranch, and now even that's gone. What are we doing here?"

A WONDERFUL NURSE named Diane Capps, a former colonel in the military and a White House nurse during the Reagan administration, came to live with the Reagans to help care for the President. Mrs. Reagan had called her in Winston-Salem, North Carolina, to see if she would come to California to assist in caring for Mr. Reagan. Diane had served in Vietnam and worshipped him, so she would be honored to. She worked her tail off, hardly ever taking a break. She never really had time to date anyone, and only occasionally she would say, "I'm going to my friend's house in Malibu for the weekend." Otherwise, she was always there.

Diane loved baseball and especially the Atlanta Braves. One of the President's golfing partners, Chase Morsey, had box seats at Dodger Stadium. When Mrs. Reagan found out that the

Atlanta Braves were going to be in town, she called me to see if I would take Diane to the game.

"Mrs. Reagan," I said, "I'd be happy to, but I don't have any tickets."

"Don't worry, John. Chase has some seats." Diane and I arrived at the stadium but had no idea where Chase's seats were. An usher escorted us down the steps inside Dodger Stadium, past rows and rows of seats. We were getting closer to the front, until we finally reached our seats—the first row behind home plate. For Diane, it was a rare break from her work.

One time when Diane, the President, and I were crossing a street together, he fell and scraped his knee. He hadn't picked his foot up when we got to the curb. I was very upset because I couldn't catch him at just that moment. When we returned home, Mrs. Reagan asked, "What happened?"

"The President fell," Diane answered. "It wasn't John's fault."

He said repeatedly that he was all right. He was more concerned about his torn trousers.

The three of us would go for walks together near the Reagan home. Although the President was becoming less verbal every week, that glint in his eyes remained for a long time. His favorite thing to do was to visit Roxbury Park in Beverly Hills. The place was brimming with nannies and small children who would be out playing in the sun. He would find a suitable park bench and sit and watch them. Even dressed down, in a sweater, and with a hat on, it wouldn't take long for someone to notice him.

Before you knew it, children were gathered around him. He would smile and laugh, the Reagan charm coming out. It was the first time I saw him playing with little children, and I could tell that he really enjoyed it. They would want to shake his hand, and some even got a hug. Whenever he spoke with someone, it was usually with a child instead of an adult. There were also those who simply wanted to take a picture of him or request an autograph. He loved to sign his name for them, but it was evident that his hand was becoming increasingly shaky.

More than anything else, he loved watching the kids play. Sometimes older kids would be there playing soccer or softball, and the ball would inevitably go out of bounds and land near the bench. He loved to kick or throw the ball back to them, and it was then that they would notice who he was. "Thank you, Mr. President!" the kids would shout.

They would go back to their game and play some more, but it wouldn't be long before someone would send the ball in his direction again, wanting him to kick it back. He would pick the ball up and ask, "You mind if I kick a goal?"

Carrying the soccer ball, he'd walk onto the field and kick it into the net. All the kids would yell "Yea!" and give him a high five.

He would take a keen interest in their games. "What's the score?" he would ask me, and I would tell him. "Oh, look at that! Good catch! What's the score now, John?"

One time Robert Shapiro, the famed Los Angeles lawyer who represented O. J. Simpson, ran into us in the park. He asked me, "Is there any way possible that I could have my grandson shake the President's hand?"

"Go get him," I said. Moments later, we went over to see the President. "Mr. President, this young man wants to say hello to you."

He stood up and said, "Oh, really?"

"This is his grandfather. Mr. Shapiro is a very busy criminal lawyer here. He's kind of on the other side." Both Shapiro and the President laughed.

Then the President looked at Shapiro's grandson. "Are you playing? Which position? I'll watch you the next time you go out there."

His pleasures were simple, just as they had always been. One warm day, I spied an ice cream truck nearby. "Would you like a Popsicle, Mr. President?"

A big grin came over his face. He was a grandfatherly figure now. "Could we?" he asked with anticipation.

I went over to the truck and ordered two Popsicles, and we sat together on the bench eating them. While I sucked mine, he consumed his with large bites. The Popsicles were the ones that are on two sticks, and you can break them in half. When he was done with his, he looked at the uneaten half of mine.

"Mr. President, would you like another?" He smiled and nodded enthusiastically. So I went and bought him another, which he also gobbled up.

One morning when we were out on a walk, the President told me directly that he needed a bathroom. He couldn't move very fast, and there were not many public bathrooms around. Knowing I needed to find one right away, I called the Secret Service office. "Contact Jimmy Stewart's house and tell them that the President needs a bathroom." His old Hollywood friend had a home just around the corner from where we were. Although the two men didn't see each other that day—Stewart was also ill—the President cheerily recognized where we were.

During his struggle with Alzheimer's, I didn't always handle things well. One morning, we were on our way to the Los Angeles Country Club for lunch and then a round of golf with his friends. We were in the limo and he asked, "Now, where are we going again?"

"We're going to have lunch at the club with friends, and then we're going to play golf." It was a short distance to the club.

Only thirty seconds had passed when he asked the same question. "Now, John, where are we going again?" I gave him the same answer. Half a minute later, he asked again . . . and again . . . and again.

This went on about ten times. I stopped saying the part about lunch because I thought that maybe he couldn't process that much information. "We're going to the golf course."

He still kept asking, and the next time I answered again, "We're going to the golf course." Finally all I said was, "We're going to golf," but I was becoming increasingly frustrated and agitated by all of this. When he tapped me on the shoulder, I turned around and sarcastically asked, "Now what?"

He just looked at me and said, "John, I know I'm upsetting you, and I realize I should know where I'm going, but I don't." I felt like such a heel. I apologized, and he said he understood.

When we arrived at the country club and got out of the limo, the President got concerned. "I know that I'm supposed to meet some people, but for the life of me I don't remember who they are."

"Mr. President," I said, "I will be right with you. I am going to walk you into the dining room, and you are going to know who they are." At that point, I did something I rarely ever did. I placed both my hands on his upper arms to reassure him that it would be all right.

As usual he said, "Okay." Still, I could tell that he was quite concerned.

We entered the dining room, and I pointed to the table where he always had lunch. "There they are, Mr. President." As soon as he looked at the table where his usual golfing buddies were waiting for him, the worried look on his face vanished.

He smiled and said, "Yes, I do know who they are." He then walked to the table by himself because the other agent and I were seated at another table. Still very upset with myself about what had happened on the way to the country club, I vowed never to let that happen again, and it didn't.

Sometimes we would stop for lunch at a hotel on the Santa Monica beach where Patti used to stay. The service was great, and the waitstaff was very kind to us. They would fight over who was going to get to serve him. After we finished our lunch, they would bring out some large cookies for dessert. President Reagan would eat his in only a few bites. Then he would look over at me and ask, "Say John, are you going to eat that cookie?"

I would smile, shrug my shoulders, and say. "I don't know, sir."

"Well, if you're going to eat it, shouldn't you eat it now?"

"I guess I'm not gonna eat it."

It was a little game we played. I was not making fun of him; it was just a game, and he knew it. He would tap his fingers on the table for a few minutes and then finally say, "Well, if you're not going to eat it, I will," and he would snatch the cookie from my plate and eat it.

I would laugh. "Good for you, Mr. President. We don't want to waste a good cookie."

Later, when we returned to the house, I told Mrs. Reagan the story. She just shook her head and smiled. "Only you."

Alzheimer's had forced the President to give up his riding and his favorite place on earth—the ranch. Now, I was being pushed to give up something I loved too. I had injured my left knee badly in the military. Following an operation, I had gone through an extensive rehabilitation regimen. The wound healed, and I was always able to pass all of my Secret Service tests. Later, I hurt the same knee when we were practicing jumping out of moving vehicles at the Secret Service's training facility in Beltsville, Maryland, but I recovered from that injury as well.

One morning in 1988, we were at the ranch and something happened that revealed my physical vulnerabilities. We were out riding on a trail, enjoying a peaceful, uneventful ride, when my horse stepped into a gopher hole. Normally when that happens, you just stay with the horse, and he will pop right back up. My horse did that, but then he stepped with his other front foot into another gopher hole. Horses usually fall down, not over. However, he was still trying to get his balance back from the first hole, and he fell onto his left side, his full weight landing on my left knee. Realizing what was about to happen, I had stuck my left foot out, attempting to get out of the saddle and out of the horse's way, but I wasn't quick enough. As my left foot touched the ground, the horse fell on me. I could literally feel a crunch.

The President and Ray Shaddick, my supervisor who was riding with us that morning, both looked on in horror. They could see that I was in pain and knew that having an eleven hundred-pound animal on top of you was horrific. Fortunately, my horse got back up and just stood there.

"Are you all right?" the President asked. "Are you all right?"

I got right up and told him that I was. "I can go on," I reassured him. In reality, that was about the dumbest thing I could have done. I rode with him for the next hour or so in incredible pain. During that time, I did further damage to the knee.

As a result of the injury, I had to have a total knee replacement surgery in September 1988. That was really the straw that broke the camel's back. My orthopedic surgeon, Dr. Richard D. Scheinberg, told me, "You are a forty-year-old man with an eighty-year-old and well-abused leg. You need a total knee replacement, and it will be three months before you can return to work." There was talk that I might not be able to work again. I called my supervisor and explained to him what had happened and that the doctor said I should recover and still be able to pass my physicals. He told me that if I thought I could stay, then I should.

Although the surgery brought me back 100 percent, the reality was starting to creep in. Secret Service agents must remain in exceptional shape. Every three months they go through a battery of physical tests to make sure they are up to the job. I had always passed the tests with flying colors, but now the injuries I had received while riding with Reagan for more than a decade were beginning to take their toll.

As an agent, you are focused and are always concerned about one thing: keeping the President safe. Rarely do you consider your own frailties. It was hard for me to have mine exposed. Another serious injury, this one to my wrist, came in 1994. The President was busy taking off his saddle, so I went over to my horse. When I reached up to take the saddle off my horse, I twisted my wrist and *snap*! You could hear the tendons break like a twig. The saddle went flying against the bell stand, and as I held my wrist to my chest, I fell backwards, landing almost next to the saddle. I scared the hell out of the horse, and he went flying too. Thank God, he didn't go near the President. The other agents thought I was having a heart attack. Because the pain was so intense, I couldn't talk for a couple of seconds to tell them what had happened.

With the help of cortisone shots over the next ten years, I was able to keep the wrist relatively functional. I continued to pass all my tests, and my marksmanship numbers at the shooting range were still very good. Unfortunately, time was not on my side. The sustained use of my wrist and the extent of the injury started to impede my shooting.

One morning in 1996, we were practicing hand-to-hand combat at the Secret Service training facility. My opponent was dressed in a padded red protective suit and a helmet with a facial mask. I was holding a baton that the Secret Service trains agents with and makes available to them. It is small, only six inches long when collapsed, making it easy to tuck into your belt, but when it is extended, it becomes more than a foot long. When I flipped my baton open that morning, I suddenly felt my right wrist snap again. The baton went flying across the room, and two people had to duck. Doubled over in incredible pain, I was having difficulty breathing.

A couple of months later, I was at our training facility again and something else happened. I was on the firing range. When I drew my weapon, my wrist snapped again, and the weapon fell. That is very dangerous. It was at that moment I had a sinking feeling that it might be over.

I had been in the Secret Service for twenty-three years. It

had been my life, and my fellow agents and the Reagans were my family. Now, that was coming to an end. The Secret Service was unforgiving about physical injuries, and rightfully so. It just had to be that way. There was no possibility of taking a "light-duty" job, since there is no such thing in the Secret Service. If a police officer is hurt, he can go on light duty. Agents, however, no matter what their job assignment, are required to be available for temporary protective duties.

I was scheduled to go before a retirement review board in Washington, D.C., in March 1997. At that time they had all my medical records to study, and I was to be given their decision concerning my future in the Secret Service. Before I went before the board, I saw Mrs. Reagan and explained to her what was happening—that I would soon find out whether I could continue in my position with the injuries I had sustained.

She asked, "If they say you can't, what happens next?"

"Mrs. Reagan, chances are that I won't be coming back as an agent."

Upset and worried, she asked. "Well, can't you just do other things?"

"No, it doesn't quite work that way, Mrs. Reagan. If a situation happened and you got hurt because I couldn't fulfill my duty, I could never forgive myself."

She said she understood, and she could also sense how upset I was. "Now I think I know how the President felt when I told him a few years ago that he couldn't ride anymore," I told her.

My hand doctors, Dennis Phelps and my Ranchero friend Hill Hastings, were on a conference call with the review board and explained where my injuries had come from, their extent, and what they meant. They didn't deliberate for very long. I was going to be retired.

I went back to Mrs. Reagan. She was taking it very hard. First, I said goodbye to President Reagan, who was deep in the pit of Alzheimer's. Then I turned to Mrs. Reagan. "A new agent will take over, and Washington has assured me that this detail will always get the best of the best." I smiled. "I'll be back, but it will be better this time. I'll be a civilian and we can really be friends." She liked that very much.

At my retirement party in Los Angeles in April 1997, Mrs. Reagan made a surprise appearance. Several Service friends from Washington, D.C., made the trip to the West Coast, and together we relived the good times. They had arranged for a government car to drive me home. As I was riding away, I wanted to send one final message. I called the Rawhide Command Post on the radio.

"Rawhide Command Post," they responded, "go ahead, sir."

"This will be my last official transmission as your supervisor. Thanks for the memories."

"Roger, sir, and thank you." I then broke down and wept.

What happened to me subsequently completely backed up the review board's findings. I have had a total reconstruction of my right wrist by Hill Hastings, who is with the Indiana Hand Center. Fortunately, because of the surgery, I have been able to go back to the thing I most enjoy—my beloved horseback riding.

I visited the Reagans numerous times after I left the Secret Service. With the exception of family members and a few close friends, Mrs. Reagan had few visitors. Always vigilant, she was working to protect the President's dignity. *How ironic*, I thought,

RONALD REAGAN

June 5, 1997

Dear John,

As your loyal riding partners for nearly two decades we insist on joining your colleagues, family and friends in congratulating you on the occasion of your retirement from the United States Secret Service. We can hardly believe you are really going to ride off into the sunset - shedding your ear piece, the dark suit and those "creative" neckties for that perfect pair of tattered cowboy boots that tell the proud stories of long ago rides.

It seems like only yesterday that you joined the President-Elect's Detail and we set off on an extraordinary journey together. Whether we were visiting foreign lands, attending to the business of the nation at the White House, or simply spending time in that weathered room out back at the Ranch just cleaning the tack -- you were with us during many of life's most significant moments.

Today, however, you begin a new chapter in your life and, while it must be bittersweet (it certainly is for us), we wish you every happiness as you realize your future on a slower trail. Sit tall in your saddle, John, for you have much to be proud of as a distinguished member of the United States Secret Service and American patriot. We will be thinking of you as you set off on your adventurous course (and we'll be wondering how often you'll come visit). God bless you.

Sincerely,

Ronald & Nancy Reagan

that this most dignified president was succumbing to an illness that
completely robs one of their dignity. Whenever I saw Mrs. Reagan,
she was always strong and never let it be known how burden-
some it must've been. Someone might have suggested that he be
cared for in a facility somewhere, but Mrs. Reagan, determined
to care for her husband, wouldn't hear of it. She didn't want to
travel or go far away for fear that he might die and that she
wouldn't be there for him in the end.

People often ask me, "Was Ronald Reagan really a cowboy?"
In today's world, some people use that term derisively. They
mean it as an expression of a gun-happy, aggressive fellow who
shoots first and asks questions later. Real cowboys, of course,
were rarely like that. Instead, they often were young men who
would go riding for six months, taking two or three horses with
them. Not only did they have to ride all day, but at night they
had to stand post to make sure that coyotes did not come down
into the camp and kill the cattle.

For the cowboy, there were also the ever-present realities of
the nineteenth century. If he fell off his horse and broke a bone,
he could die, since the nearest doctor might be a few weeks away.
Cowboys got infections from handling horses and cattle, and
there was the possibility that gangrene might set in. Their teeth
rotted, and since there was no dentist or Novocain, someone
would just rip a tooth out with pliers. They ate beans and hard-
tack, and with a good rancher, they might make thirty dollars a
month. It was a grueling existence.

Men who wanted to become real cowboys lived by an unoffi-
cial code. Since it was an unforgiving way of life, they needed to
take responsibility for their mistakes. They didn't gloat when they
were right, because next time they might be wrong. Furthermore,

their word was always their bond. A handshake was all it took to close a deal. Cowboys lived a life of devotion to their horses and to their cattle. They were sworn to protect them.

Ronald Reagan wasn't a cowboy. However, he did possess some of the same inner principles. He always meant what he said. His words became his deeds, and he lived a life devoted to his beliefs, his family, and his country. To him, there was nothing greater than the power of the individual and his or her ability to make a difference. He liked the ideal of heroism, and he believed people from all walks of life were heroes. He believed that communism was evil and that it could be defeated. In the end, it was defeated, and the man who never wanted the credit deserved it. He had the cowboy spirit.

13

The Ending

June 5 was a glorious morning until I received the news. I was on a weekend ride with thirty-five guys on the Chamberlin Ranch in Los Olivos, just fifteen miles from the Reagan Ranch, and we had finished our morning ride. Per our custom, we had maintained no contact with the outside world since the previous day. However, a friend of mine on the ride, Jack Wilson, went to his truck to check on something. When he turned the ignition key, his radio came on and he heard the announcement of the passing of President Reagan. He came running to me and said, "John, have you heard the news?"

Without asking, I knew what he meant.

"Ronald Reagan has just passed away," he said.

I had been expecting it to come soon, but who knew what "soon" was? A torrent of emotions flooded through me, but I took comfort in the fact that I was riding my horse when the news finally came. I looked up toward the sky and said to President Reagan, who was now with the angels, "This is how you wanted it—me on a horse—isn't it?"

Despite knowing that his death was bound to come, it hit me hard, so I did what most people do to cope: I got busy. Over the past few years, dozens of news organizations had contacted me to ask if I would be willing to do interviews when President Reagan passed away. I had agreed, and it was now time, so I took the saddle off my horse and smiled faintly to my friends, who had gathered around. "I've got to go," I told them, "they will be looking for me." Before I left, a couple of the guys came over to console me.

I jumped in my truck and headed toward home. While in my truck, I called Young America's Foundation Executive Director Floyd Brown to ask if there had been any calls. The foundation had purchased the Reagan Ranch and is preserving it for future generations. I had asked all the news organizations to make their requests through them. Dozens of interviews were already lined up. They wanted me to come straight to their office to begin, but I told them that I needed some time alone first. I took care of my horse and then went home and took a shower before heading off for the onslaught.

During the course of the next twenty-four hours, I did interviews with CNN, C-SPAN, ABC, NBC, CBS, Fox News, the *Today* show, *Good Morning America*, a dozen newspapers or more, and plenty of radio programs. While I was going through the flurry of interviews, my emotions made it difficult for me to keep things straight. "Who am I talking to again? What time is that interview?" In the Secret Service, keeping track of schedules had been a critical ingredient of the job, but with the pain and hurt running through me, I felt completely lost in everything.

Instinctively, I wanted to stay close to the ranch, the place the President loved. A producer from the *Today* show called and said they wanted to fly me to New York for an extensive interview. "I'm not going anywhere," I responded. The reporters usually asked the same questions. One thing, however, that did surprise me was the number of reporters who told me off camera how much they had liked President Reagan, even if they had disagreed with his politics.

ABC's *Good Morning America* asked me to do an interview at the ranch. I didn't want to go up there, because I thought I might lose my composure entirely, but Floyd convinced me to do it. Kate Snow was the interviewer, and she was very gracious. While the crew was setting up the lights, I looked around the ranch where I had spent so much time in the company of the President and Mrs. Reagan. Tears welled up in my eyes, and I had to walk away. Later, I rejoined Kate after I had gathered myself.

I received an invitation to attend the funeral at the National Cathedral in Washington, D.C., and I had a quick decision to make. All the seating for the funeral service was assigned, and I was humbled that I had been selected to sit one pew from Mrs. Reagan. I was also informed that I was on the so-called VIP List, which meant I had access to all the events, including going to the Reagans' house after the funeral, but I just couldn't do any of it. Besides, I knew that there were people who would take care of Mrs. Reagan. She had so many friends and the Secret Service who were with her now, and I didn't want to bother her. I called Charlie Kinnel, the agent in charge of the detail, and asked him how she was doing.

I watched from a safe distance—alone and in my home. In retrospect, it was a mistake, because I spent a lot of time crying. At one point, I pulled out my collection of photos, which made my emotions run even deeper.

The procession that carried the casket to the U.S. Capitol building was solemn, yet befitting, for a man I had grown to love and respect. When I saw the four horses pulling the casket and the lone horse with the President's boots on backwards, signifying the riderless horse, it was a particularly poignant moment for me. He had spent so much of his lifetime on the back of a horse. Now his boots were all that were left to put in the stirrups. That night at my house, I held his hat and ran my fingers over the spurs and boots that he had worn for twenty years and had then given to me after he stopped riding.

As the people lined up by the thousands for the viewing in the U.S. Capitol rotunda, I was struck by how they all stood there patiently, people from all different walks of life. A friend who had served on the PPD called to tell me that they had arranged for a special private access viewing for all the agents who had protected President Reagan. I later received another call from a member of the Secret Service. After seeing my interviews, the assistant director called and said, "You represented the Secret Service very well." That meant more to me than just about anything else.

I kept looking at Mrs. Reagan as I watched the funeral service from my home in California. My heart just ached for her. He had been her life partner and soul mate for more than fifty years. She had been expecting his death, but not really preparing for it. Now that it was here, she could not quite bring herself to accept it yet. For her, the whole experience was exhausting. When she boarded the plane for the flight back to California and the evening graveside service, she was tired, but could not sleep.

While I decided against attending the funeral at the Washington Cathedral, I would go to the smaller, more private burial ceremony at the Reagan Library. That afternoon I drove from Santa Barbara to Simi Valley, the mountaintop site of the Ronald Reagan Presidential Library. From the airport to the Library, where his body would be laid to rest, the streets were thronged with citizens who wanted to see the fortieth President's flag-draped coffin on its way to the final hilltop. There were tens of thousands of people lined along the way. Some held their hands over their hearts as the casket passed by, others cried. There were more, however, who applauded and cheered a man they had grown to love. The California fire departments had pulled out their hook and ladder trucks and positioned them on the overpasses along the route. They configured the ladders in a way that made a pyramid and then draped them with huge American flags. All the firefighters were standing and saluting as the Reagan motorcade went through.

When I finally arrived at the Library, there were thousands more people outside watching the mourners gather. About seven hundred personally invited guests were there for the burial. Many of those outside were ordinary Americans who had come to get a glimpse of the coffin. I asked one man, "Why are you standing out here in the hot sun waiting for the President's body to come by?"

He looked at me and said, "I want my kids to see a real hero, to be a part of history, and to remember this day when a great man was honored like no other."

I had made sure that two of my friends, J. J. Quinn of the United States Navy and Steve Chelander of the United States Air Force, who were President Reagan's military aides, were able to attend the ceremony, and I met them outside of the Library. They had asked me in advance, "What should we wear?"

"Your uniforms," I told them. They are all retired now and out of the service, but the President would have been proud to see them dressed like that again. When they saw the casket, they saluted him with tears in their eyes. He was still their commander in chief.

The people at the graveside service included family members, longtime friends, old golfing buddies, and former political advisors. There was also a phalanx of members of the news media, who had set up booths to cover the funeral. The networks had approached me about interviews at the ceremony, but I said no. I was still swimming pretty deeply in my emotions.

When we took our places outside the Library, I was sitting a few rows back from the front in an aisle seat. This gave me a great opportunity to see many friends, but what struck me most was how old all his friends had become. Where had the time gone? How had it moved so quickly? Why did I only seem to notice it now?

We were there to mourn the passing of a great man, but during the evening there were also many warm hellos between old friends. It was so wonderful to see people with whom I had worked so closely but had not seen in years. When I ran into Diane Capps, his longtime nurse, who was now living in North Carolina, I gave her a long, solid hug. "Thanks for taking care of him all those years," I said, my voice breaking.

As the late afternoon turned to evening, I could tell that all that had happened was taking a toll on Mrs. Reagan. We all knew that President Reagan's passing was the best thing for both of them, but when it came time for the service to end, she literally did not want to let go of the casket. She was touching it gently, not wanting to leave. "I can't believe he's gone," she kept repeating. "I can't believe he's gone." She was finally free of the burden of caring for him—but she didn't want to be. Finally, members of the family had to take her away.

As the ceremony ended at sunset (something the President had requested), the Navy jets flew overhead in the missing-man formation. While I was looking out over the panorama near the hillside where the President was laid to rest, I heard the clicking of hooves down below. Along a path nearby, I spotted several mounted police from the sheriff's department riding. "Well," I said, "you've done it again." It was as if the President had managed in some mystical way to see to it that horses and riders had made it to his burial ceremony.

President Reagan is gone, but memories of him will remain in the hearts of millions. I'm very fortunate because I *really* knew the man. I often look back at the great opportunity I had to be so close to him, and when I have to make a decision about life or deal with a problem, I ask myself, *What would he have done?* I think he made me a better person. While I cannot see him anymore, there is still a living part of my relationship with him that I can visit to this day. The last horse he rode, Sergeant Murphy, is still alive and lives in a sun-bathed, five-acre pasture in the Santa Barbara area. There you will find him playing and frolicking with my horse, Monty.

Acknowledgments

Any book includes substantial contributions from those whose names do not appear on the cover. In my case, I have literally dozens of colleagues from my years in the Secret Service that I could mention, and loads of friends who have been a help and encouragement over the years.

In particular, I would like to thank Dennis Ayers and Ralph Pfister of the U.S. Park Police. Dennis taught me how to ride a real horse properly and showed tremendous dedication to President Reagan. Ralph made all those rides hauling horses back and forth to Camp David so enjoyable.

Dennis LeBlanc and Barney Barnett, two early members of the Reagan team, worked the ranch before Ronald Reagan became President. Dennis offered invaluable help and friendship during my tenure at the Reagan ranch. Barney made hard work a pleasure, and his devotion to President Reagan was contagious.

Bill Clark, President Reagan's longtime friend and trail partner, was always ready to give me advice and guidance when I asked for it. Our rides together are special. Doug Herthel, a personal friend and veterinarian to both President Reagan's and my horses, made everyone's job easier.

I met Si Jenkins when I made my first trip to Santa Barbara to work the ranch. He gave me invaluable advice and has become a great friend. Doug and Sally Taylor helped by sitting down for hours to talk about the old days and bringing back so many memories. Gary Wooten was helpful with information about President Reagan's earlier ranches.

The Reagan Ranch is now in the hands of the Young America's Foundation; Ron Robinson and Floyd Brown have become close friends. Working with them has been a joy—the ranch could not be in better hands. Floyd in particular deserves credit for badgering me to write this book, and it would not have been written if not for his constant encouragement. I also want to thank Floyd's talented wife, Mary Beth, for her contributions.

Thanks also to Kathy Osborne, personal secretary to the President; Rick Ahern, personal assistant to the President; and Joanne Drake, President Reagan's last Chief of Staff. All three were critical in providing stories, memories, or assistance in bringing this project to a successful conclusion.

White House photographers Pete Sousa, Bill Fitzpatrick, and Mary Ann Falkelman kindly gave me many wonderful photos.

Several books were helpful in providing background information and accounts of Ronald Reagan's life before he was president. These include Lou Cannon's *Governor Reagan*, Peter Hannaford's *Ronald Reagan and his Ranch*, Anne Edwards' *The Reagans: Portrait of a Marriage,* and Paul Kengor's *God and Ronald Reagan: A Spiritual Life*.

Beginning this literary venture introduced me to a whole new world. I was guided by my friend Nelson DeMille, a best-selling novelist who took time to give me his valuable advice about writing a book, and my literary agent, Joe Vallely. Michaela Hamilton, my editor at Kensington Books, believed in this project from the beginning and made it happen.

Rochelle and Peter Schweizer helped to put my words to paper and were patient with me as the manuscript took shape. They came to understand the language of the Secret Service and horses.

Finally, I want to thank Ronald and Nancy Reagan for all our wonderful years together.

Index

239